Music
of the
Baroque

Music of the Baroque

An Anthology of Scores

Second Edition

DAVID SCHULENBERG

New York • Oxford
OXFORD UNIVERSITY PRESS
2008

Oxford University Press publishes works that further Oxford University's
objective of excellence in research, scholarship, and education.

Oxford   New York
Auckland   Cape Town   Dar es Salaam   Hong Kong   Karachi
Kuala Lumpur   Madrid   Melbourne   Mexico City   Nairobi
New Delhi   Shanghai   Taipei   Toronto

With offices in
Argentina   Austria   Brazil   Chile   Czch Reublic   France   Greece
Guatemala   Hungary   Italy   Japan   Poland   Portugal   Singapore
South Korea   Switzerland   Thailand   Turkey   Ukraine   Vietnam

Copyright © 2008 by Oxford University Press, Inc.

Published by Oxford University Press, Inc.
198 Madison Avenue, New York, New York 10016
http://www.oup.com

Oxford is a registered trademark of Oxford University Press

ISBN 978-0-19-533116-5

Printing number: 9 8 7 6 5 4 3 2 1

Printed in the United States of America
on acid-free paper

Contents

PREFACE

This is an anthology of scores to accompany *Music of the Baroque*, a study of European music from the late sixteenth through the mid-eighteenth centuries. The present volume can also be used independently as a collection of study scores. Although editions of most of these works can be found in academic music libraries, less well-endowed collections are likely to lack scores even for major works, and an anthology of this nature may prove a valuable acquisition for smaller libararies.

The present edition adds or substitutes new works by Lalande, Gaultier, Frescobaldi, Froberger, Rossi, Castello, Biber, Legrenzi, Torelli, and C. P. E. Bach. New editions are provided for works by Monteverdi (*Orfeo*), Strozzi, Gabrieli, J. S. Bach (Cantata 127), Jacquet de La Guerre, Couperin, and Marini. In addition, the selections from Lully's *Armide* have been expanded and the unsatisfactory early edition of its overture replaced by a new score.

A complete discussion of each work, including its historical and cultural context, biographical material on its composer, and analysis, is in the accompanying volume. The present volume gives not only the score but the verbal text of each vocal work (with translation, where necessary), commentaries on the edition used and on any performance issues raised by the work, and information about the work's sources. The accompanying volume includes plot summaries and other supplementary material, much of it in the form of tables and boxes readily distinguished from the main text for easy reference.

The music selected for presentation comprises complete works and musically self-contained excerpts. The few exceptions, such as the ornament tables extracted from several French Baroque sources (Selection 29), are self-explanatory. Where excerpts rather than complete works are given, as with operas, an effort has been made to present a coherent portion of each work, such as a series of successive scenes. In several cases, additional, briefer extracts appear in the text volume in the form of musical examples.

This anthology includes a number of "noncanonical" selections, including works by women composers, alongside familiar standards. Also present are a few pre- and post-Baroque selections to illustrate the opening and closing chapters of the text volume, which provide transitions to music from other historical periods. The commentaries point out specific features of each score, such as any significant editorial emendations or notable aspects of notation. They also mention important issues of performance practice raised by each work. Translations are as literal and preserve as much of the original syntax as possible.

A word about the editions used is appropriate. A greater number of works are presented in new scores than in the first edition. But no apology is needed for the fact that the present volume retains editions reprinted from other sources, an expedient dictated by the need to present a broad variety of compositions in an affordable format. This feature can be turned to an advantage in a study collection, for a musician or music historian must be familiar not only with various types of recent editions—which differ significantly from one another in physical appearance and editorial policy—but also with facsimile reprints from older editions and from original sources. The commentaries accompanying the scores will assist readers in understanding the diverse types of edition that are increasingly available and, indeed, indispensible for anyone studying, performing, or listening to European music of the past.

All of the editions reproduced here employ modern notation, and only a few use unfamiliar "old" clefs for certain parts. A few facsimiles from original printed sources employ clef and note shapes somewhat different from those in current use, but experience has shown that students have little difficulty in adjusting to this. Moreover, the experience of having done so empowers them to make practical use of a much wider variety of sources than would otherwise be the case.

Where works appear here in new editions, the musical and verbal texts have been established wherever possible through comparison with primary sources. Although it is impractical for a volume of this nature to include a formal text-critical apparatus, an effort has been made to identify the most important editorial emendations in the commentaries or in the scores themselves. In particular, editorial accidentals and other small additions that might be open to question are set in brackets. Time signatures, beaming of small note values, and other aspects of original notation have been modernized, but otherwise editorial alterations have been limited to those necessary for study purposes; ornaments, figured bass symbols, and other performance-related markings have been left largely as in the sources.

Music
of the
Baroque

1. Giovanni Pierluigi da Palestrina (1525/6–1594),
Dum complerentur (motet)

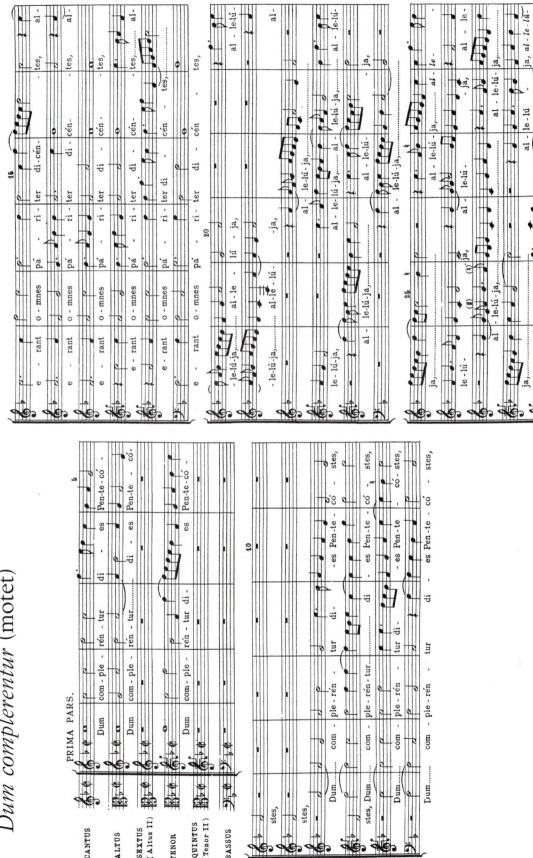

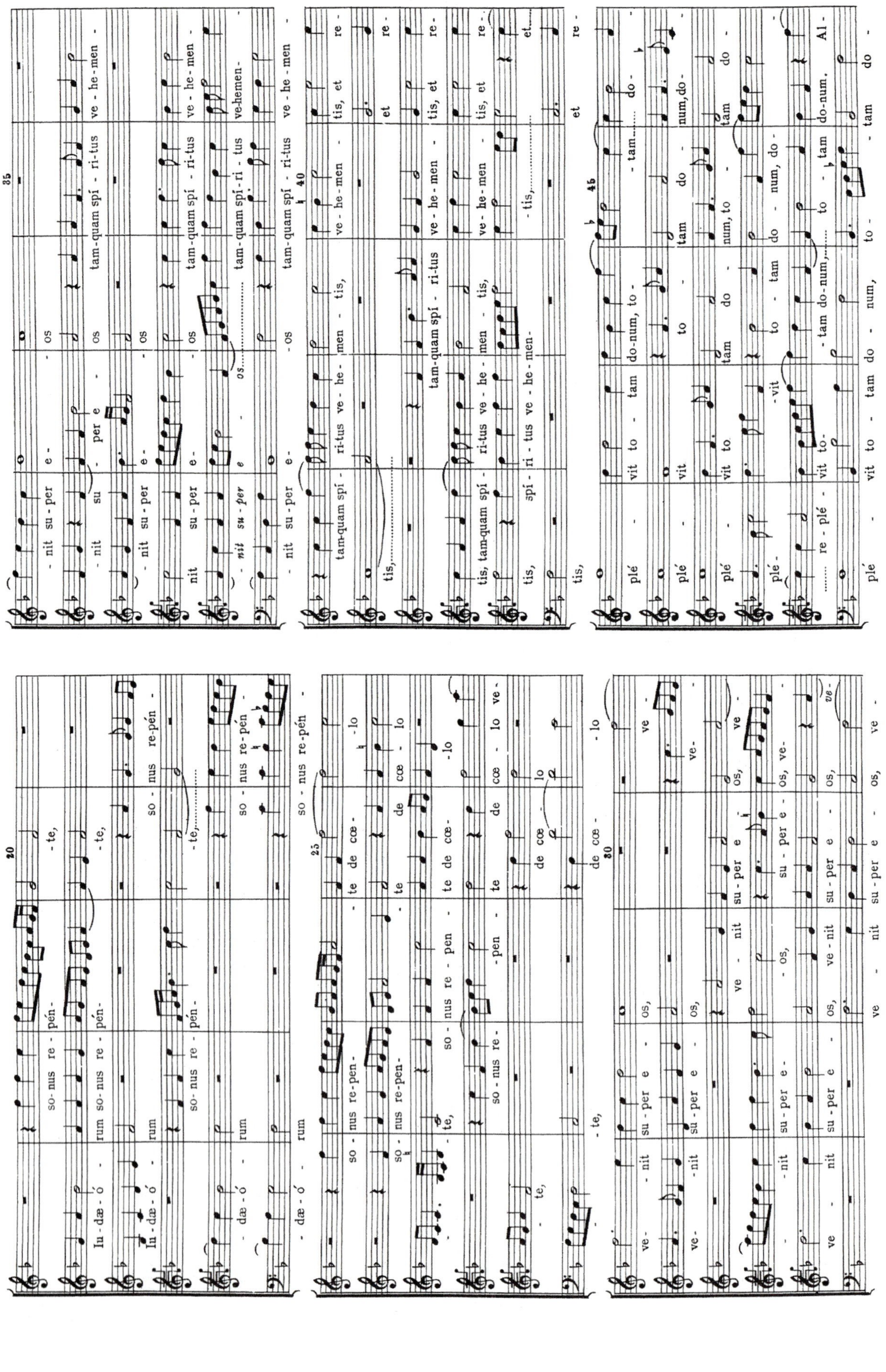

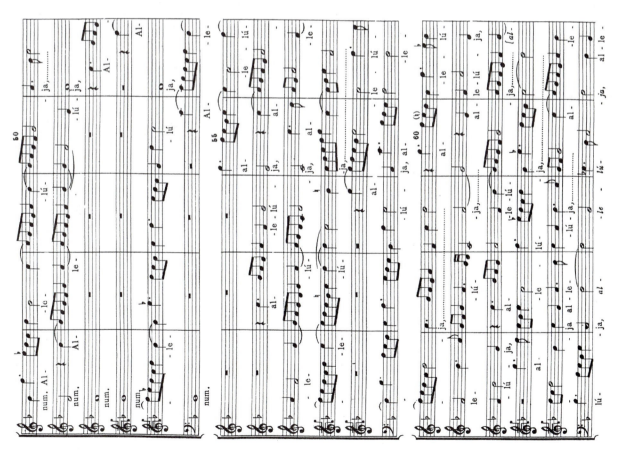

TEXT AND TRANSLATION

Prima pars

1 Dum complerentur dies Pentecostes,
2 erant omnes pariter dicentes alleluja,

3 et subito factus est sonus de coelo,
   alleluja
4 tamquam spiritus vehementis,
   et replevit totam domum, alleluja.

Secunda pars

5 Dum ergo essent in unum discipuli
   congregati,
6 propter metum Iudaeorum,
7 sonus repente de coelo venit super eos,

8 tamquam spiritus . . .

—Acts 2:1–2, with additions

Part 1

When the feast of Pentecost was come,
all [the disciples] were together, saying
hallelujah,
and suddenly a sound was made from heaven
   —hallelujah!—
as from a rushing wind, filling
the entire house—hallelujah!

Part 2

Thus, when the disciples were gathered
   together as one
because of fear of the Jews,
a sound from heaven suddenly came over
   them,
as from a wind . . . .

EDITION

Like most modern scores of sixteenth-century music, this edition has been prepared from the individual vocal parts in which the work originally circulated. The layout in score is the work of a modern editor, as are the addition of barlines and other elements of notation necessary for presentation in score.

At the beginning of the score, the six parts are labeled with the names given them in Palestrina's original printed edition. Also shown are the original clefs, which differ from those used in the modern edition except in the top part. The editor has also suggested modern equivalents (given in parentheses) for the original labels *sextus* and *quintus*.

In the text, the editor has added accent marks to indicate syllables that would receive a stress when spoken aloud. Some repeated words and phrases of the text are printed in italics (*like this*). These represent editorial additions; in the original printed edition, not all repetitions of words were written out.

Accidentals placed above the notes, such as the natural in the quintus part in measure 11, are editorial suggestions. Commonly referred to today as *musica ficta*, these editorial accidentals correspond in most cases to alterations that singers probably would have made in performance in Palestrina's day.

A few instances of slurs occur in this edition (as in the tenor, mm. 25–26). These correspond with *ligatures* in the original notation (discussed below under Selection 2); they probably have no practical significance for the performer.

PERFORMANCE ISSUES

The question of what types of voices should be used, or how many should sing each part, cannot be settled by examining the score. The editor has suggested that the sextus part be sung by a second alto, but modern performers must decide whether this means a boy or girl alto, an adult female alto or contralto, or an adult male falsetto singer. In Palestrina's performances at the Sistine Chapel in Rome, adult men probably sang all six parts. Instrumental participation, although banned in the Sistine Chapel, might have taken place in performances elsewhere.

Closely related to the issue of voices and instruments is that of original pitch. The modern concept of a fixed, absolute pitch (a' = 440 Hz) did not exist in Palestrina's day; thus, regardless of the notated pitches, in practice the actual pitch level of any work might have been higher or lower than what we would assume. There is some evidence that purely vocal music such as this motet was usually sung at Rome at a significantly lower pitch than the notation would indicate to us.

The score provides no indications of dynamics, tempo, or other aspects of musical interpretation now deemed essential to performance. As noted above, the accent marks in the text are editorial. Palestrina's music tends to set these accented syllables on higher or longer notes, or with melismas; thus, these syllables do not require an additional stress accent as well. Other issues for performers to consider include the pronunciation of the Latin text and the addition (if any) of improvised ornamentation and embellishment, a common practice in Palestrina's time although not necessarily employed in all works. Modern performers resolve these issues based on their understanding of historical performance practice and their analysis of the score. In addition, many decisions, now as in Palestrina's day, must depend on the circumstances of an individual performance: whether the latter takes place in a large church, a small private chapel, or a concert hall—the latter being a uniquely modern venue for a sacred motet of the Renaissance.

SOURCES

The score has been reproduced from *Le opere complete di Giovanni Pierluigi da Palestrina*, ed. Raffaeli Casimiri, vol. 5 (Rome: Fratelli Scalera, 1939), 149–58. The work was originally published in Palestrina's *Liber primus . . . motettorum* (Rome: Dorico, 1569); this edition is based on the reprint of 1600 (Venice: Scotto).

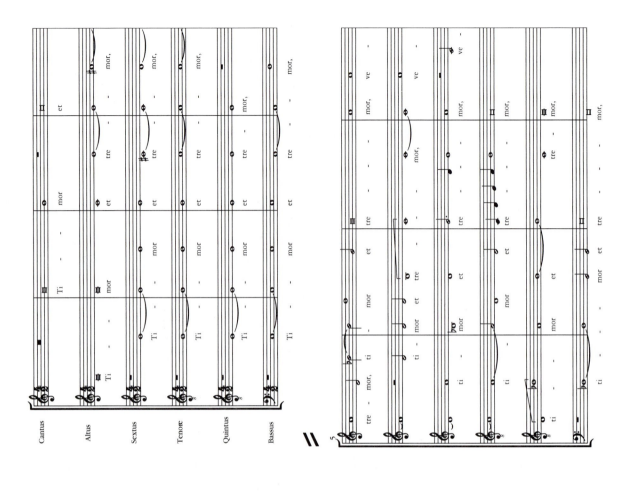

2. Orlande de Lassus (1530/2–1594),
Timor et tremor (motet)

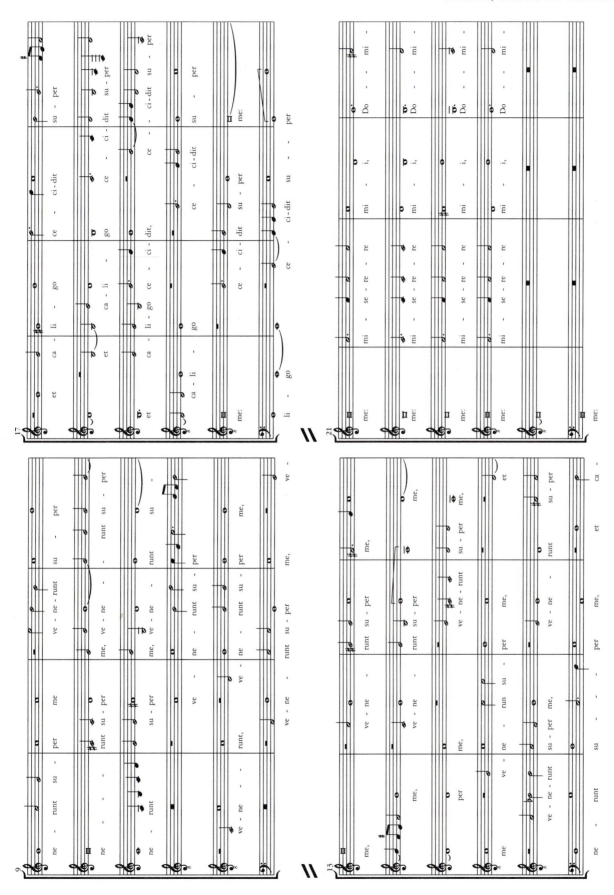

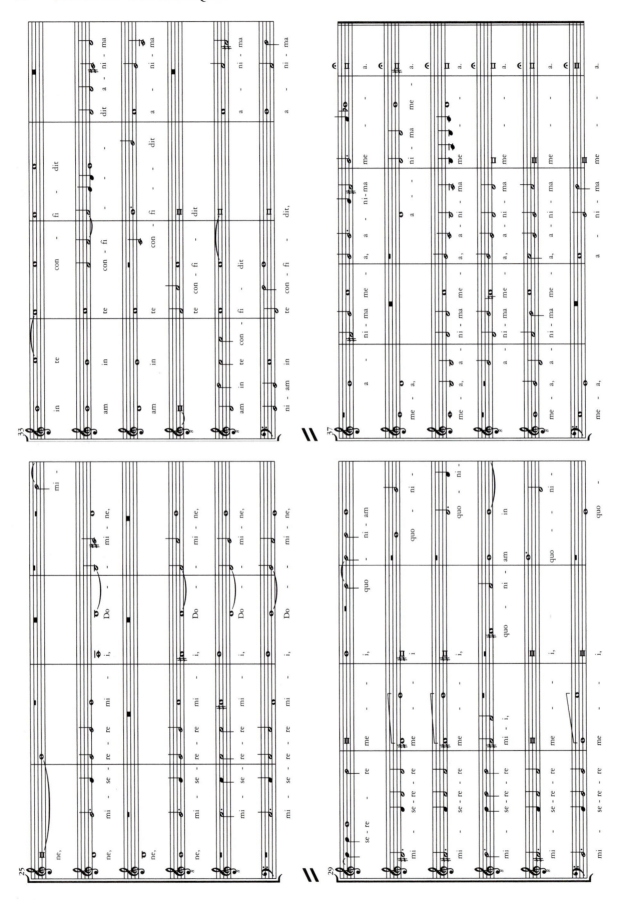

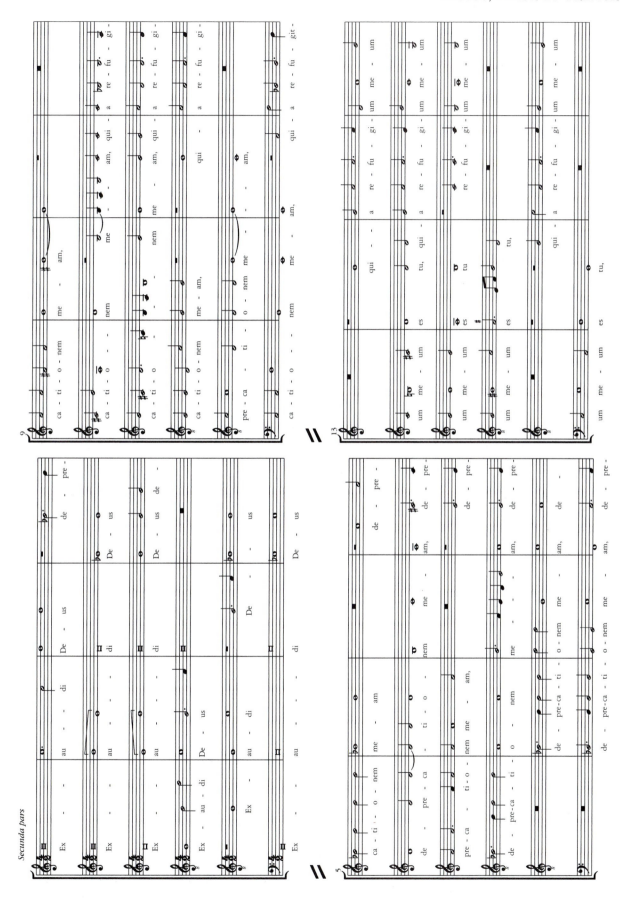

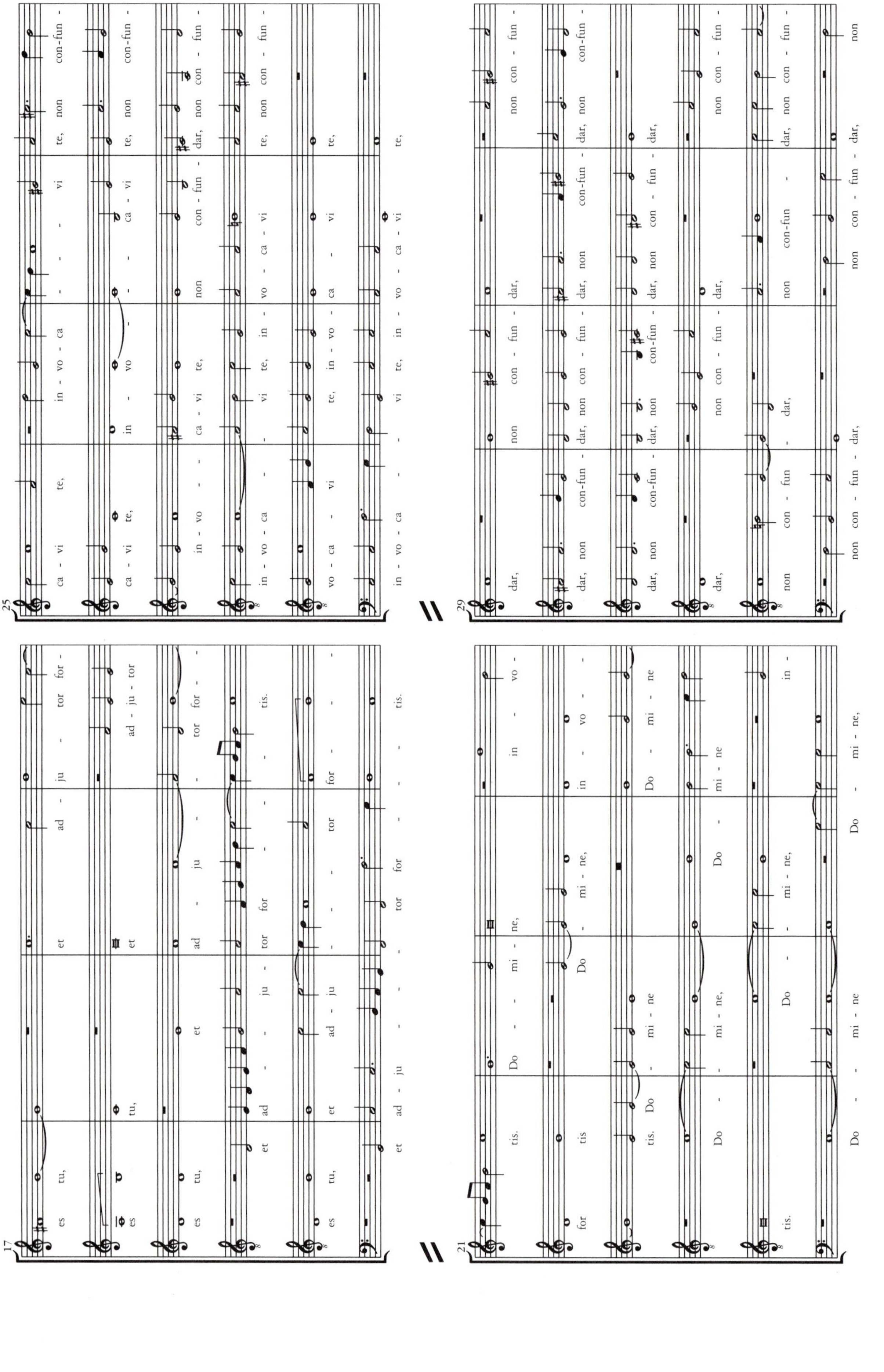

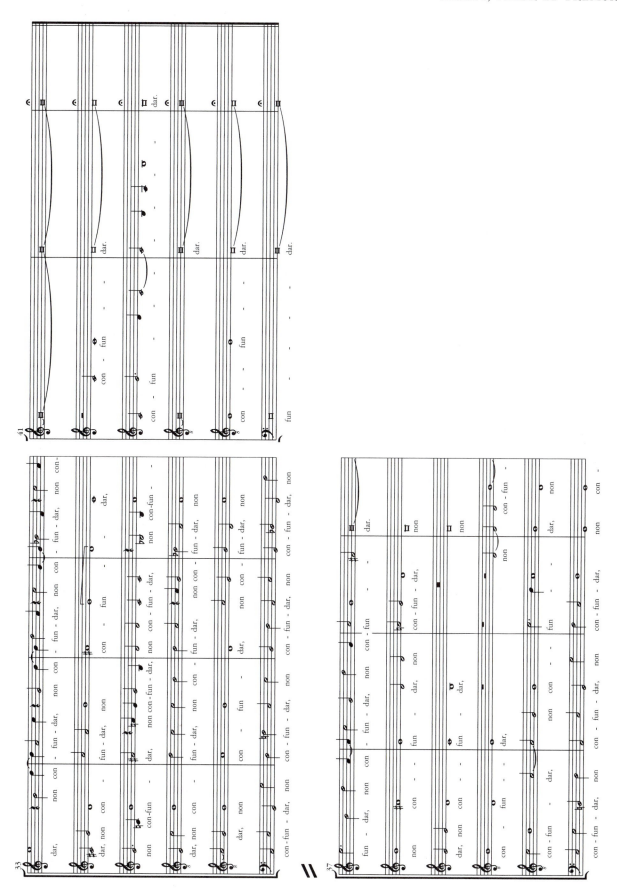

TEXT AND TRANSLATION

Prima pars

1 Timor et tremor venerunt super me
2 et caligo cecidit super me.
3 Miserere mei, Domine,
4 quoniam in te confidit anima mea.

Seconda pars

5 Exaudi Deus deprecationem meam,
6 quia refugium meum es tu et adjutor
   fortis.

7 Domine, invocavi te,
8 non confundar.

—From Psalm 54:1, 5, 6

Part 1

Fear and trembling have come over me,
and darkness has fallen on me.
Have mercy on me, Lord,
for in you trusts my soul.

Part 2

Hear, God, my prayer,
for you are my refuge and my strong helper.

Lord, I have called on you;
do not confound [me].

EDITION

Our edition is again a modern transcription of an early printed edition in the form of individual vocal parts. The score resembles that of the Palestrina work (Selection 1), reflecting the general similarities in style and notation between the two motets. Nevertheless, modern editors do not always present similar compositions in similar ways, and the present score differs in some ways from that of the Palestrina work.

For example, this score lacks editorial indications for accentuation in the Latin text. More significantly, it gives the notes in their original rhythmic values; in the Palestrina score, each note is shown in half the value of the original print. The Lassus score thus contains a preponderance of whole notes and half notes, whereas the Palestrina score comprises mainly halves and quarters. The Lassus score even contains some instances of the *breve*, a square note shape in common use during the Renaissance but rarely seen today; it is equivalent to two whole notes (as in the first note of the altus part). These large note values might suggest a slow tempo to a modern performer, but in fact this motet was probably performed at roughly the same tempo as the Palestrina motet; that is, a whole note here has approximately the same duration as a half note in the Palestrina score.

A few of the longer notes in this score are joined together by brackets, as in part 1, measure 5 (quintus). Like the slurs in the Palestrina score, each bracket indicates the presence in the original of a *ligature*: a special symbol used as shorthand for two or more separate notes, usually of relatively long duration. A holdover from medieval notation (in which they were used far more frequently), ligatures were falling out of use during the sixteenth century. They may sometimes have functioned somewhat as slurs do in later music; in sixteenth-century music, the notes of a ligature are almost always sung to a single syllable.

PERFORMANCE ISSUES

This work raises much the same questions of performance as does Selection 1. The composer is more likely to have envisaged instrumental participation in this work, but purely vocal performance remains equally possible. The large rhythmic values of the present score do not imply an unusually slow tempo, despite the seriousness of the text. The present notation implies placing the beat on the whole note, and any needed changes in tempo are written into the music: the initial motion predominantly in whole notes leads to lively movement in smaller values by the end of part 2.

SOURCES

Our score is based on the edition in Orlando di Lasso, *Magnum opus musicum . . . Theil X*, ed. Franz Xaver Haberl, *Sämtliche Werke* 19:6–9. Haberl's source was the *Magnum opus musicum* (Munich, 1604), a posthumous compilation of Lassus's works.[1]

---

[1] For a modern edition based on the first printing of this work, in *Thesauri musici tomous tertius* (Nuremberg: Montanus and Neuber, 1564), see *Orlando di Lasso: The Complete Motets 3*, edited by Peter Bergquist, Recent Researches in the Music of the Renaissance, vol. 132 (Middleton, Wis.: A-R Editions, 2002).

3. Don Carlo Gesualdo, Prince of Venosa (ca. 1561–1613), *Beltà, poi che t'assenti* (madrigal)

TEXT AND TRANSLATION

1 Beltà, poi che t'assenti,	Beauty, since you have consented,
2 Come ne porti il cor, porta i tormenti.	As you carry off my heart take also my torments.
3 Che tormentato cor può ben sentire	For a tormented heart can well feel
4 La doglia del morire,	The pain of dying,
5 E un'alma senza core	But a soul without a heart
6 Non può sentir dolore.	Cannot feel sadness.

EDITION

Unlike Selections 1 and 2, Gesualdo's madrigals appeared not only in printed partbooks but in score, a rare form of publication for this type of music.[2] Gesualdo's score includes barlines, but in keeping with the practice of the time these were placed irregularly, creating measures of varying length. The present score follows Gesualdo's barring; thus, for example, measures 20–22 are only half as long as those at the beginning. In modern terms the time signature at the opening should be $\frac{4}{2}$, changing to $\frac{2}{2}$ at measure 20. The original meter sign (₵) has nevertheless been left at the beginning of the score; the value of the notes remains constant throughout the composition.

Otherwise the modern edition raises few issues not already encountered. One small point involves the Italian text, in which certain vowels are joined by curved lines or bows. These markings indicate the presence of **elision** (or *synaloepha*): the combination of adjacent vowels into a single sound, forming one syllable where there might otherwise be two or even three. Elision is an important device in Italian poetry, since elided syllables are counted as one for the purposes of prosody (poetic meter).

PERFORMANCE ISSUES

This score remains, in principle, purely vocal. The secular text would, at the time of composition, have permitted the use of female as well as male adult singers. The difficulty of singing the chromatic progressions in tune suggests that Gesualdo had professional singers in mind, possibly accompanied by lute, harp, or harpsichord, as was the case with performances by the "Three Ladies" of Ferrara, for whom works such as this might have been intended. Such performers would undoubtedly have added improvised ornamentation, although this particular score leaves little room for elaborate embellishment.

Like Selection 2, this score contains a built-in accelerando, opening with relatively large note values but concluding with predominantly smaller ones. Hence it is possible to maintain a fairly steady beat throughout the madrigal, although performers might employ ritards at the ends of phrases (as in m. 4) and push forward when the rhythm flows more swiftly in quarter notes. Despite its publication in score, performances of this music were probably from independent part books, without a conductor; this would have made extreme or sudden changes of tempo difficult to coordinate without extensive rehearsal.

The chromatic progressions raise the issue of tuning and temperament. Modern singers, accustomed to accompaniment on the equal-tempered piano, often overlook the possibility of alternative tuning systems or *temperaments*. But Gesualdo and his

---

[2]Parts: *Madrigali a cinque voci, libro sesto* (Naples: Carlino, 1611); score: *Partitura delli sei libri de' Madrigali a cinque voci*, ed. Simone Molinaro (Genoa: Pavoni, 1613).

contemporaries knew many different tuning systems, some of which would have deepened the expressive effects of his chromatic progressions. For example, in certain temperaments the chromatic half step sung by the soprano at the outset (g′–g♯′) is smaller than the diatonic half step that follows (g♯′–a′). The lute, which might have participated in performances of this work, is in principle an equal-tempered instrument, like the modern piano. But other temperaments would have been used on the harp or the harpsichord, and Gesualdo and his Ferrarese patrons must have known of special keyboard instruments with extra keys (to distinguish, e.g., G♯ from A♭) that would have been useful in training and accompanying singers in this type of music.

4. Claudio Monteverdi (1567–1643),
Luci serene (madrigal)

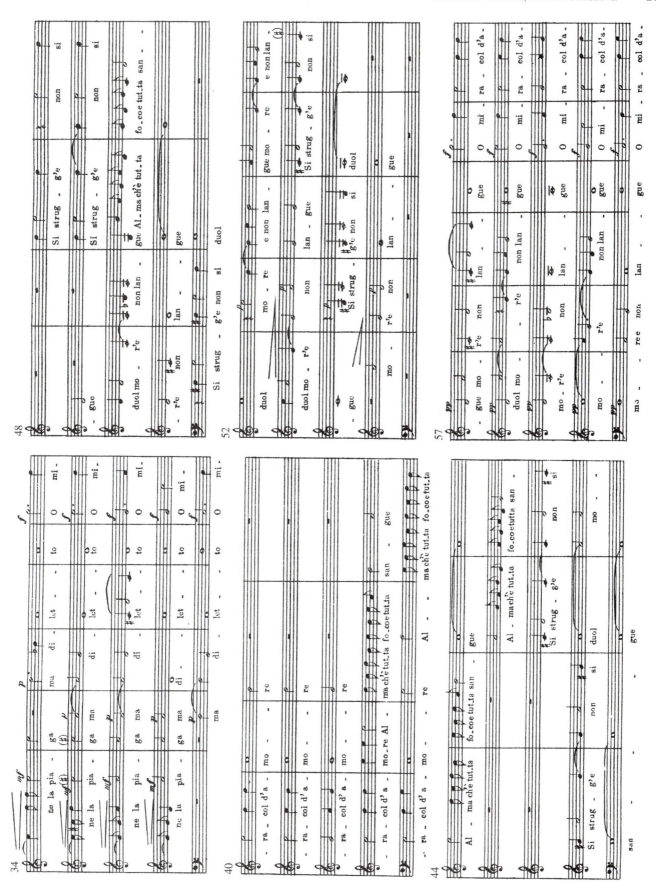

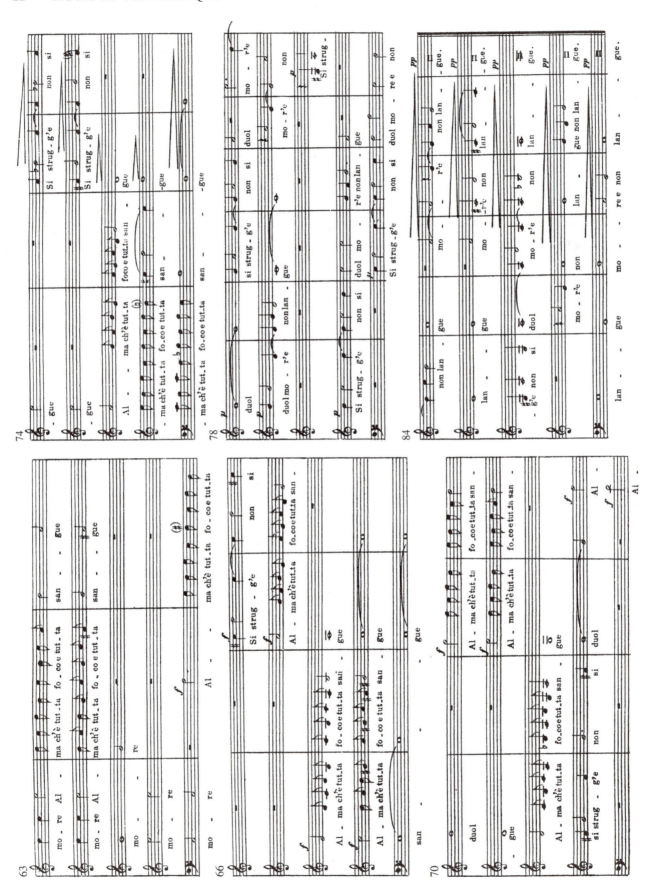

TEXT AND TRANSLATION

1 Luci serene e chiare,
2 Voi m'incendete, voi, ma prov'il core
3 Nell'incendio diletto, non dolore.

4 Dolci parole e care,
5 Voi mi ferite, voi, ma prov'il petto
6 Non dolor ne la piaga, ma diletto.

7 O miracol d'amore:
8 Alma ch'è tutta foco e tutta sangue
9 Si strugg'e non si duol, muor e
     non langue.

—Ridolfo Arlotti

Eyes serene and clear,
You inflame me, you, but my heart feels
In burning delight, not pain.

Sweet words and dear,
You pierce me, you, but my breast feels
Not pain in the wound, but delight.

Oh, [such a] miracle of love:
That a spirit that is all fire and all blood
Is consumed but does not suffer, dies but
     does not languish.

EDITION

Our score is based on the individual vocal parts of Monteverdi's Fourth Book of Madrigals. An edition from the earlier twentieth century, it includes editorial dynamic markings such as **mf** (*mezzoforte*) in measure 1 and the crescendo symbols in measures 13–16. Also editorial are the tempo marking (*andante*), all parenthesized accidentals, and the occasional slurs (as in mm. 7 and 9), although the latter serve only to mark melismas. The clefs used for the original printed parts are shown in parentheses at the opening.

Two wrong notes in the edition must be corrected: in measure 5, note 1 of the basso should be A, not G; in measures 86–87, the tied note in the canto should be a′, not f′.

PERFORMANCE ISSUES

Like the preceding work, this madrigal may have been conceived with instrumental participation in mind. Indeed, two of the many seventeenth-century reprints of this work included an instrumental accompaniment in the form of a basso continuo part, that is, a bass line for a keyboard or other instrument on which the player improvised chords, guided by numbers and other symbols written above the notes.[3] Although often described today as optional, such parts may have reflected the usual practice of the time.

The editorial dynamic markings in our edition are arbitrary additions, but Monteverdi probably expected singers to employ dynamic contrasts in response to the changing emotional character of the text. The editor's *andante* marking is somewhat misleading; the tempo throughout should probably be such that the eighth notes beginning in measure 42 are lively enough to represent the image of "fire" present in the text at that point. As in Selection 3, changes of pacing are written into the music, although some freedom of tempo was no doubt taken for granted.

SOURCES

This edition is reproduced from *Tutte le opere di Claudio Monteverdi*, ed. Gian Francesco Malipiero, vol. 4 (Asola, 1927). The source for the latter was Monteverdi's *Quattro libro de madrigali* (Venice, 1603).

---

[3]The basso continuo part appeared in an edition published in 1615 in Antwerp (in modern Belgium); it is included in *Claudio Monteverdi: Madrigali a 5 voci: Libro quinto*, ed. Elena Ferrari Borassi, *Opera omina*, vol. 5 (Cremona: Fondazione Claudio Monteverdi, 1974), 128–33.

5. Giulio Caccini (1551–1618), *Sfogava con le stelle*
(continuo madrigal)

le - i, Men-tre co-tan-to ar-de - te I vi - vi ar-do - - - - - ri

mie - i.   La fa-re-ste col vo-stro au-reo sem-bian-te Pie-to-sa si,   pie-to-sa si,   co-

11 #10 14   ♭   ♮

- me me fa - - te a-man - te,   La fa-re-ste col   vo-stro au - reo sem-bian-te Pie-to-sa

6   6   11 #10 14

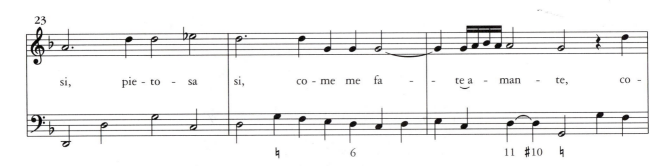

si,   pie-to - sa   si,   co-me me fa - - te a - man - te,   co-

♮   6   11 #10 ♮

Trillo

- me me fa - - - - - - te a - man - te.

6 6   ♮   #10 11   11 #10 14

TEXT AND TRANSLATION

1 Sfogava con le stelle	To the stars, under the nighttime sky,
2 Un infermo d'amore,	A lovesick man
3 Sotto notturno ciel il suo dolore,	Poured out his sadness
4 E dicea fisso in loro:	And said, his eyes fixed upon them:
5 O, immagini belle	"O lovely images
6 Del idol mio ch'adoro,	Of my idol whom I adore,
7 Sì come a me mostrate,	Just as you show me,
8 Mentre così splendete	By shining so splendidly,
9 La sua rara beltate	Her rare beauty,
10 Così mostraste a lei,	Show her
11 Mentre cotanto ardete	That, as strongly as you burn
12 I vivi ardori miei.	Are my own hot flames.
13 La fareste col vostro aureo sembiante	Make her, through your golden semblance,
14 Pietosa sì, come me fate amante.	As merciful as you make me ardent."

—Ottavio Rinuccini

EDITION

This edition is based closely on the original printed score. The notation has been updated only by changing sharps to naturals where modern notation employs the latter.

PERFORMANCE ISSUES

Caccini left no indication of the type of voice or instrument(s) to be used, despite his inclusion of a lengthy preface on the intended manner of singing.[4] The preface furnishes many suggestions for the singer, especially with regard to ornamentation. Although Caccini has written out all necessary melodic embellishments, or *passaggi*, especially the melismas at measures 14 and 26, he expects singers to add small ornaments, such as the *esclamazione*—an expressive swell on a long note, as on "O" in m. 6—and the *trillo* (one instance of the latter is notated, in m. 27).

Caccini's figured bass differs from later examples in its use of compound figures; for example, measure 25 uses the numerals 11–10 where later composers would have written 4–3. Other editions provide written-out realizations of the figured bass. However, it is practically impossible to notate a stylish realization of this figured bass for the theorbo, the preferred continuo instrument of the time, or for the harp and lira da braccio, two other continuo instruments that Caccini played.

In any case, the character of the realization would vary depending on whether it was played on theorbo, archlute, or another instrument. But Caccini's reference to a "simple string instrument" for the accompaniment implies that the realization itself should be simple as well, lacking independent melodic counterpoint except where the figures call for it, as in measures 2 and 4 (see the example below). The compound figures shown there, like the use of tied bass notes to indicate the precise rhythm of the realization, are rare in later figured basses. A number of contemporary publications give general guidelines for figured bass realization, but many issues remain uncertain; written-out realizations in contemporary sources vary in their approach. The example below illustrates two possible ways of realizing the opening phrase on a keyboard instrument, the first

---

[4]For a translation, see the edition by H. Wiley Hitchcock (Madison, Wis.: A-R Editions, 1970), which also includes a realization of the figured bass.

doubling the voice, the second remaining beneath it (in either case, a harpsichordist would break or arpeggiate most chords, perhaps also restriking tied notes that have died away).

It is quite certain that Caccini did not expect the bass line to be doubled by a melodic instrument (such as the viola da gamba); such doubling became customary only much later.

SOURCE

This edition is based on the original edition of Caccini's *Le nuove musiche* (Florence, 1601), available in facsimile (New York: Broude, 1973).

6. Claudio Monteverdi (1567–1643), *Orfeo*, Act 2 (opera: selections)

a. Sinfonia and two arias: "Ecco pur ch'a voi ritorno" and "Mira ch'a se n'alletta"

pur ch'a voi ri-tor-no Ca-re sel-ve_e piag-gie_a-ma-te Da quel sol fat-te be-a-te Per sui

b. "Mira, deh mira Orfeo" through chorus, "Ahi, caso acerbo"

199
A ri-ve-der le stel - le;   O se cio ne-ghe-ram-mi_em-pio de-sti - no   Ri-mar-rò te-co

205
in com-pa-gnia   di mor - te.   A dio ter-ra,   a dio
Farewell earth   farewell

211
cie - lo,   e so - le   a di - - o.
heavens   sun,   farewell

241

li - ta, a gran sa - li - ta il pre-zi-pi... il- pre-ci -- pi-zio_è pres - so. -

a gran sa - li - ta il pre-zi - pio il pre-zi - pio è pres - so.

li - ta, a gran sa - li - ta il pre-zi - pio è pres - - so.

TEXT AND TRANSLATION

Orfeo

Ecco pur, ch'à voi ritorno,
Care selve e piagge amate,
Da quel sol fatte beate
Per cui sol mie nott'han giorno.
*Questo ritornello fu suonato di
dentro da un clavicembano, duoi
chitaroni, & duoi violini piccioli
alla francese.*

Pastore

Mira ch'à se n'alletta
L'ombra Orfeo de que'faggi,
Hor che'nfocati raggi
Febo da ciel saetta.

Sù qual'herbosa sponda
Posianci, e in varii modi
Ciascun sua voce snodi
Al mormorio de l'onde.

. . .

Mira, deh mira, Orfeo, che d'ogni
  intorno
Ride il bosco e ride il prato,
Seguì pur co'l plettr'aurato
D'addolcir l'aria in si beato giorno.

Messaggiera

(un organo di legno & un chit{arone})

Ahi caso acerbo, ahi fat'empio e
  crudele
Ahi stelle ingiuriose, ahi ciel avaro.

Orpheus

Here I am, returning to you,
Dear woods and beloved country
Who are blessed by the same sun
By whom my nights are made days.
*The following ritornello was played
backstage by a harpsichord, two
large lutes, and two small violins
in the French style.*

Shepherd

See how Orpheus is enticed
By the shade of these beech trees,
As Phoebus [the sun god] shoots
Burning rays from heaven.

On this grassy shore
Let us rest, and in varying ways
Let each blend his voice
With the murmuring of the waves.

. . .

See, ah see, Orpheus, that all around you

The forest and the meadow laugh;
Go on with your golden plectrum,[5]
Sweetening the air on this lovely day.

Messenger

*(accompanied by a wood-pipe organ and a large
  lute)*

Ah, bitter fortune; ah, cruel, pitiless fate;

Ah, unjust stars; ah, envious heaven.

---

[5]A plectrum is a pick used to pluck an instrument such as a lute.

Pastore

(un clavic{embalo} & viola da bracio)
Qual suon dolent'il lieto dì perturba?

Messaggiera

Lassa, dunque debb'io
Mentre Orfeo con sue note il ciel
   consola
Con le parole mie passargli il core?

Pastore

Questa è Silvia gentile,
Dolcissima compagna
De la bell'Euridice: ò quanto
   è in vista
Dolorosa: hor che fia? deh,
   sommi Dei
Non torcete da noi benigno
   il guardo.

Messaggiera

Pastor, lasciate il canto,
Ch'ogni nostr'allegrezza in doglia
   è volta.

Orfeo

Donde vieni? ove vai? Ninfa,
   che porti?

Messaggiera

A te ne vengo, Orfeo,
Messaggiera infelice
Di caso più infelice e più funesto.

La tua bella Euridice . . .

Orfeo

  Ohimè, che odo?

Messaggiera

La tua diletta sposa è morta.

Orfeo

  Ohimè.

Messaggiera

In un fiorito prato,
Con l'altre sue compagne,
Giva cogliendo fiori
Per farne una ghirlanda à le sue
   chiome,
Quand'angue insidioso
Ch'era fra l'erbe asconso
Le punse un piè con velenoso dente,
Ed ecco immantinente

Shepherd

(accompanied by harpsichord and a {bass} violin)
What sad sound disturbs this happy day?

Messenger

Alas, must I,
While Orpheus charms heaven with his
   notes,
Pierce his heart with my words?

Shepherd

This is noble Sylvia,
Sweetest companion
Of the beautiful Euridice; oh, how her face is

Saddened—what has happened? Ah, great gods,

Do not turn from us your benevolent gaze!

Messenger

Shepherd, cease your song,
For all our happiness to sadness has turned.

Orpheus

From where do you come? where are you
   going? Nymph, what [news] do you bring?

Messenger

I come to you, Orpheus,
An unfortunate bearer
Of tidings [even] more unfortunate and
   unhappy.
Your beautiful Euridice . . .

Orpheus

  Oh no, what do I hear?

Messenger

Your beloved bride is dead.

Orpheus

  Ah, no!

Messenger

In a flowery meadow,
With her companions,
She was wandering, gathering flowers
To make a garland for her hair,

When a treacherous snake
That was hidden in the grass
Struck her foot with poison fangs,
And at once

Scolorissi il bel viso e ne'suoi lumi
Sparir que'lampi, ond'ella al sol fea
  scorno.
Allhor noi tutte sbiggottite e meste
Le fummo intorno richiamar
  tentando
Gli spriti in lei smarriti
Con l'onda fresca e co'possenti
  carmi;
Ma nulla valse, ahi lassa,
Ch'ella i languidi lumi alquanto
  aprendo
E tè chiamando, Orfeo,
Dopò un grave sospiro
Spirò fra queste braccia, ed io rimasi
Piena il cor di pietade e di
  spavento.

Her lovely face grew pale, and in her eyes
Grew faint the light by which the sun was
  outshone.
Meanwhile we, all terrified and sad,
Were about her, trying to bring

Her lost senses back to her
With cold water and powerful incantations;

But nothing worked, alas,
And at length, opening her fading eyes

She called for you, Orpheus,
Then, with a deep sigh,
Perished in these arms, and I am left
With my heart full of pity and fear.

Pastore

Ahi caso acerbo, ahi fat'empio
  e crudele
Ahi stelle ingiuriose, ahi ciel avaro.

Shepherd

Ah, bitter fortune; ah, cruel, pitiless fate;

Ah, unjust stars; ah, envious heaven.

Pastore [secondo]

A l'amara novella
Rassembra l'infelice un muto sasso,

Che per troppo dolor non può
  dolersi.

[Second] Shepherd

At this bitter news
The unhappy one [Orpheus] seems like a
  mute gravestone,
Afflicted with so much grief that he cannot
  grieve.

Pastore

Ahi, ben havrebbe un cor di tigre
  o d'orsa
Chi non sentisse del tuo mal pietate,
Privo d'ogni tuo ben, misero amante.

Shepherd

Ah, one would have to have the heart of a
  tiger or a bear
Not to feel pity for your misfortune,
Deprived of your beloved, wretched lover!

Orfeo

(un organo di legno e un chitarone)

Tu se' morta, mia vita, ed io
  respiro?
Tu se' da me partita
Per mai più non tornare, ed io
  rimango?
Nò, che se i versi alcuna cosa
  ponno
N'andrò sicuro à più profondi
  abissi,
E, intenerito il cor del rè de
  l'ombre,
Meco trarròtti à riveder le stelle
O se ciò negherammi empio destino
Rimarrò teco in compagnia di morte.
A dio terra, à dio cielo, e sole, à dio.

Orpheus

(accompanied by a wood-pipe organ and a large
  lute)
You are dead, my life, and I breathe?

You have left me,
Never to return, and I remain?

No, if my verses have any power,

Surely I will go to the deepest abysses

And, softening the heart of the king of
  shades [the dead],
Will lead you with me again to see the stars.
But if pitiless fate denies me this,
I will remain with you in the company of death.
Farewell, earth; farewell, heaven; and, to the
  sun, farewell.

Coro	Chorus
Ahi caso acerbo, ahi fat'empio e crudele,	Ah, bitter fortune; ah, cruel, pitiless fate;
Ahi stelle ingiuriose, ahi ciel avaro.	Ah, unjust stars; ah, envious heaven.
Non si fidi, huom mortale,	Trust not, mortal man,
Di ben caduco e frale	In good fortune, fleeting and frail,
Che tosto fugge, e spesso	Which quickly disappears; often
A gran salita il precipizio è presso.	A great cliff lies near a peak.

—Alessandro Striggio

EDITION

This edition has been newly prepared from the published score of 1609. The designations of instruments are translated (somewhat speculatively; see below) from the headings in the first edition.

PERFORMANCE ISSUES

Despite the presence of a list of instruments and headings that describe aspects of the work's first performances, Monteverdi's score raises many difficult questions. For example, it is not clear exactly to what instruments some of the terms refer. Moreover, some instrumental parts are left unlabeled (as in the sinfonia that opens Act 2), and the score fails to specify whether the vocal parts of the choruses were sung by soloists or by a larger group, or whether they were doubled by instruments. The singers presumably included women as well as men, but precisely what types of voices were is not always certain; for example, the music of the second shepherd was originally printed in alto clef, suggesting either a high tenor voice or a falsetto.

Beyond these basic issues of scoring there are the usual questions about pitch, tempo, dynamics, improvised ornamentation, and the realization of the basso continuo, which is largely unfigured. To these we can add many other questions arising from the fact that this was a stage work. For example, how large was the room in which the work was originally performed, and how did its size influence the style and volume of the singing and playing? What sort of lighting and costumes were employed, and did these influence the musical performance in any way? Where did the players sit and how were the vocal and instrumental ensembles directed and coordinated? (The score indicates that some of the instrumental music was heard from behind the scene.) What types of stage movement, including dance, did the soloists and chorus use: was it stylized or realistic? Did soloists reinforce their vocal projection through vigorous physical gestures, or were the latter restrained? Questions such as these have been carefully considered by performers as well as scholars; some modern performances have attempted to recreate elements of early practice, shedding new light on aspects of the work, but many proposed solutions must remain speculative.

SOURCE

The score is based on a facsimile of the first edition (Venice, 1609); several performing editions are available.[6]

---

[6]See, e.g., *Monteverdi: L'Orfeo: Favola in Musica, 1607* (King's Music, Redcroft, Banks End, Wyton, Huntingdon, Cambridgeshire PE17 2AA, United Kingdom, 1993).

7. Claudio Monteverdi (1567–1643), – *Strong harm. based off Plato*

Il combattimento di Tancredi e Clorinda   *Stile Concitato*

(*balletto* or dramatic madrigal)

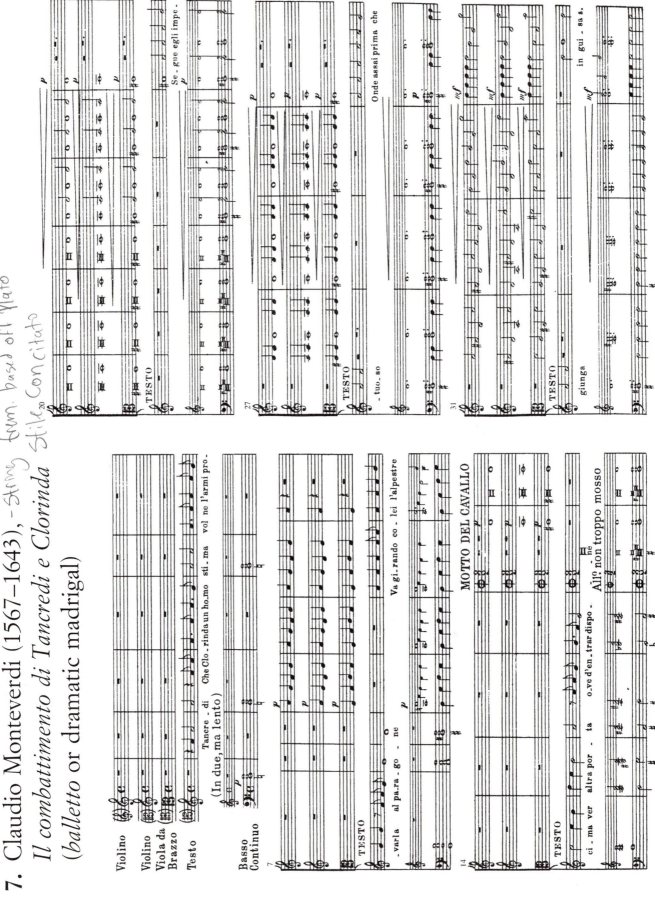

44

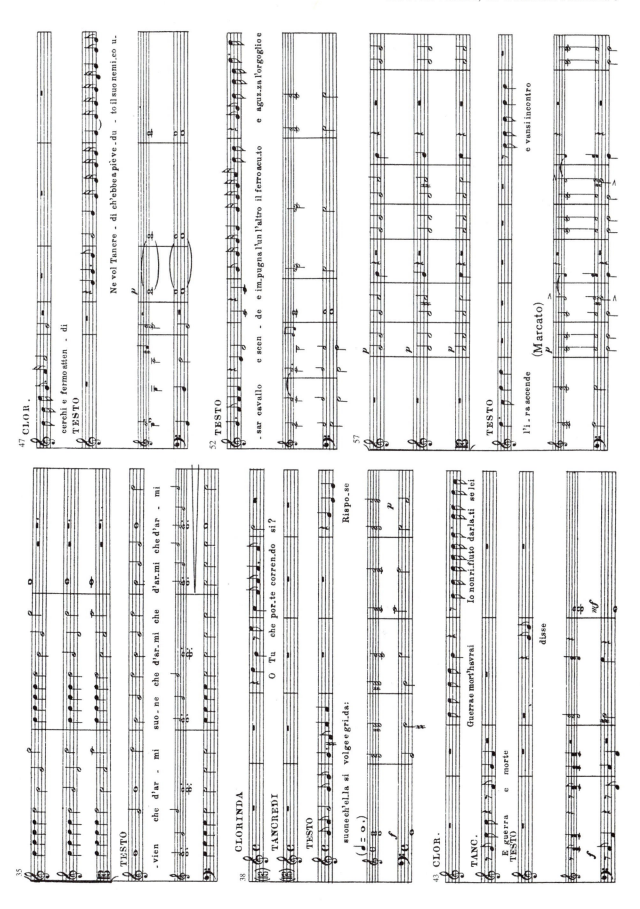

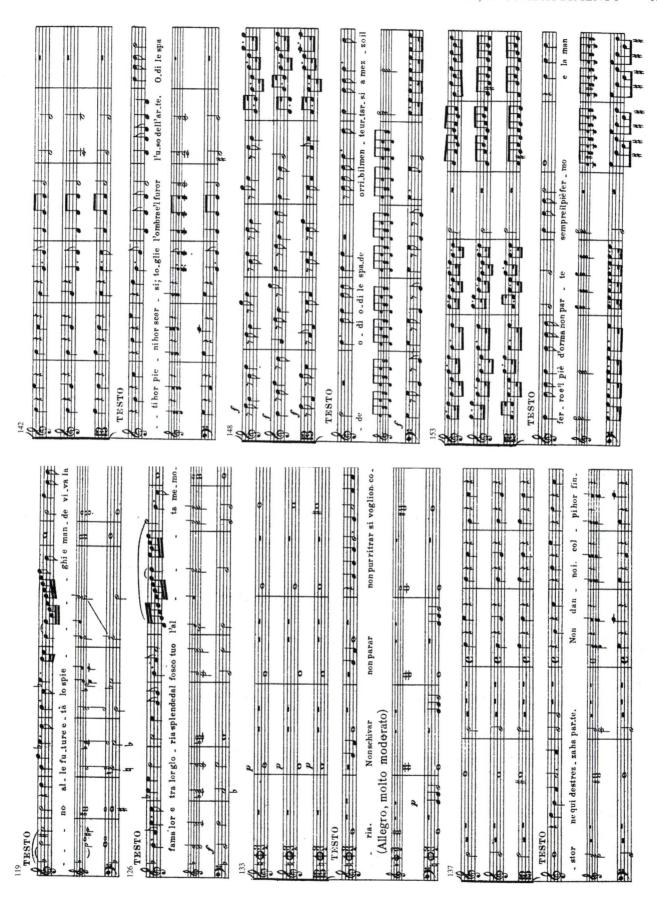

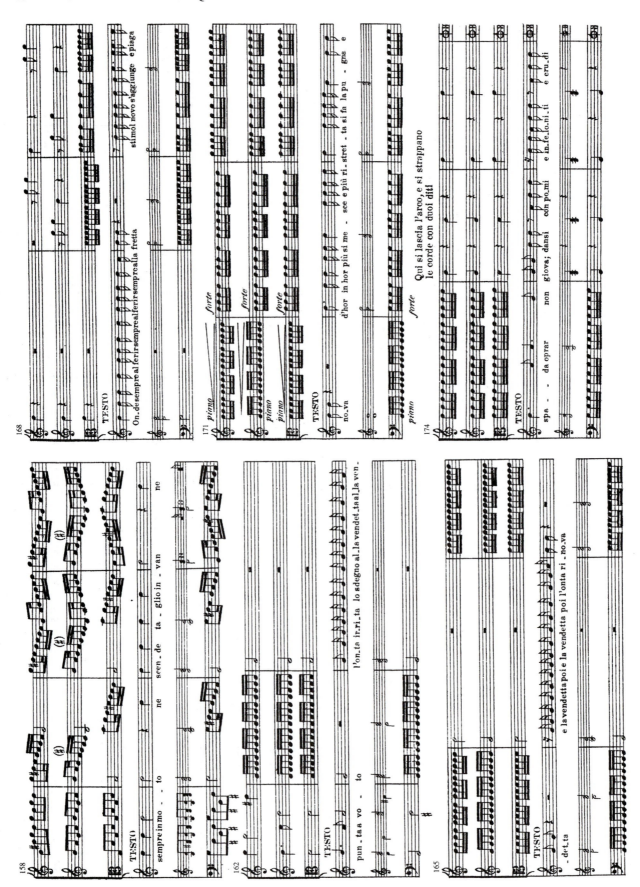

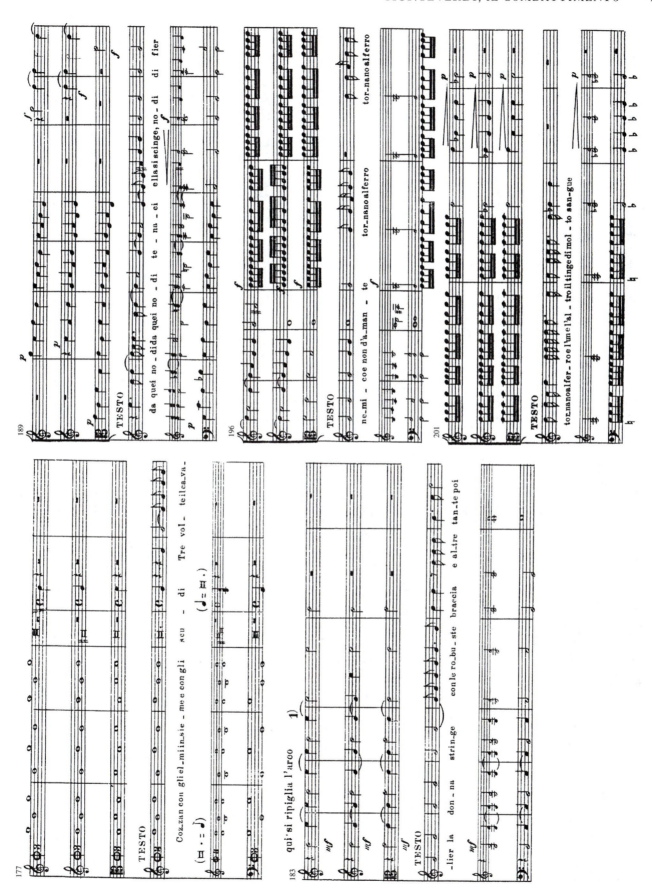

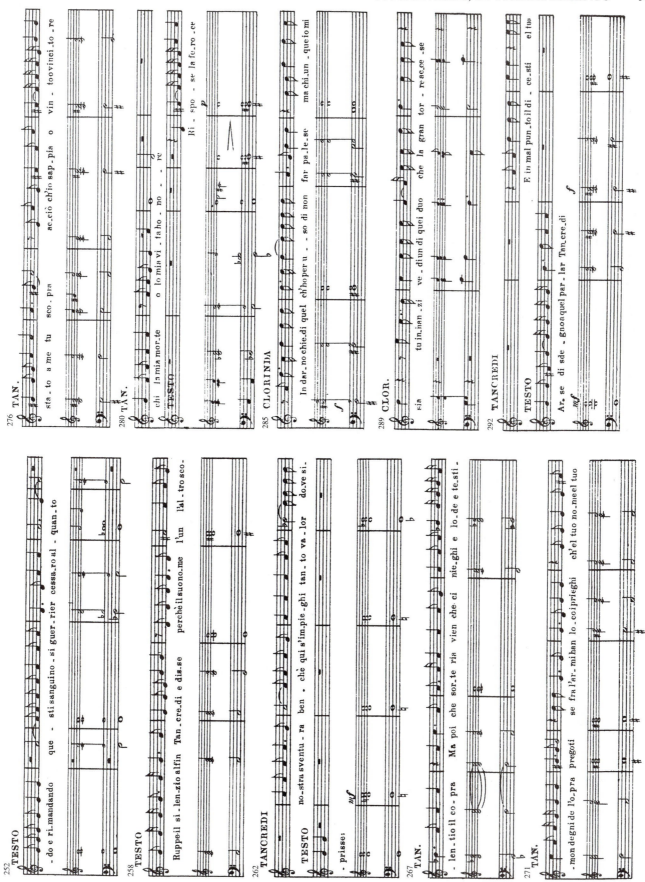

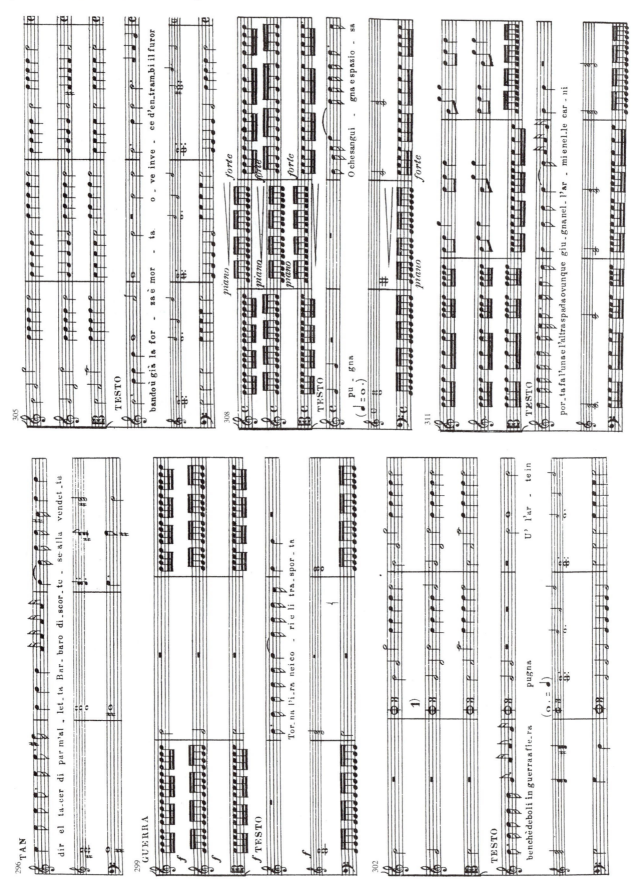

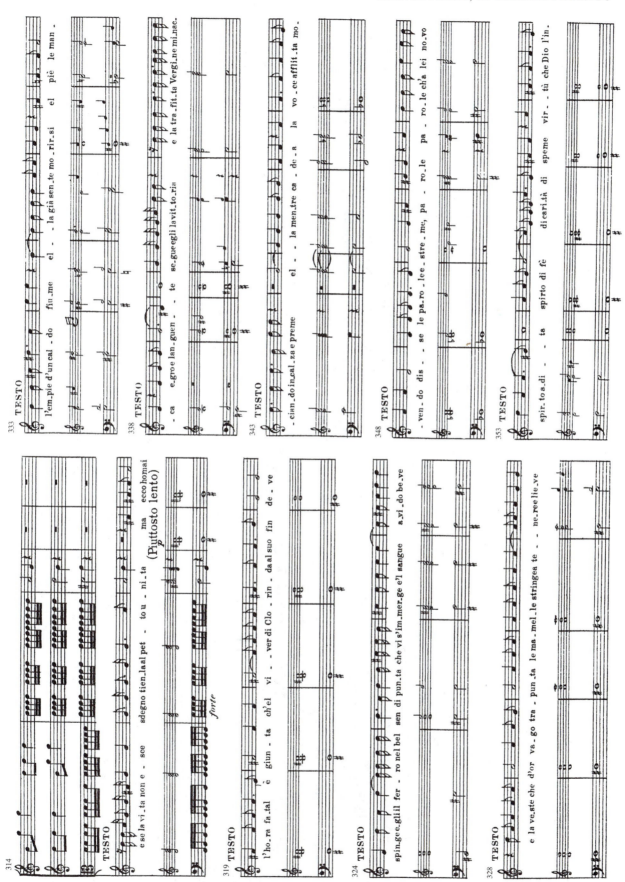

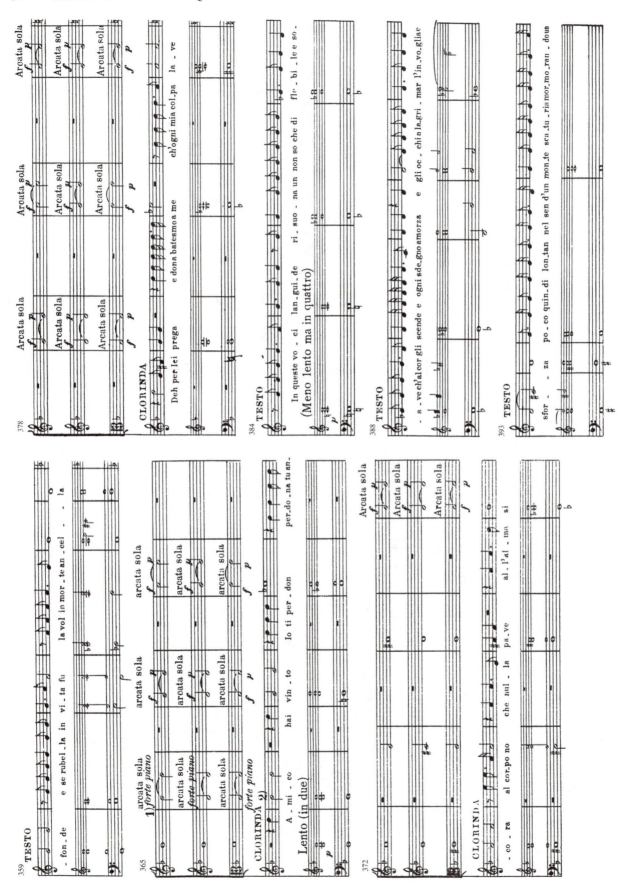

Il fine del Tancredi

TEXT AND TRANSLATION

I.

1 Tancredi, che Clorinda un uomo stima,
2 Vol ne l'armi provarla al paragone.
3 Va girando colei l'alpestre cima
4 Ver altra porta ove d'entrar dispone.
5 Segue egli impetuoso onde assai prima
6 Che giunga in guisa avvien che d'armi suone,
7 Ch'ella si volge e grida: "O tu, che porte
8 Correndo sì?" Rispose: "E guerra e morte."

1 Tancredi, thinking Clorinda to be a man,
Wishes to test her in combat.
She wanders about the rocky peak
Toward another gate that she may enter.
He follows her so impetuously that before
He reaches her his armor clatters,

So that she turns and cries: "You, what do you bring,
Running so?" He replies: "War and death!"

II.

1 "Guerra e mort'havrai," disse.
"Io non rifiuto
2 Darlati se la cerchi;" e fermo attende.
3 Nè vol Tancredi, ch'ebbe a piè veduto
4 Il suo nemico, usar cavallo, e scende,
5 E impugna l'uno e l'altro il ferro acuto
6 Ed aguzza l'orgoglio e l'ira accende.
7 E vansi incontro a passi tardi e lenti
8 Quai due tori gelosi e d'ira ardenti.

"War and death you will have," she says.
"I do not refuse
To give it to you, if you seek it," and stopping, she waits.
Tancredi does not wish, seeing his enemy
On foot, to use his horse; he dismounts,
And each seizes his sharp sword,
Whetting his pride, his anger igniting.
And they advance upon one another with steps slow and heavy,
Like two bulls jeaous and with anger burning.

[Sinfonia]

III.

1 Notte, che nel profondo oscuro seno
2 Chiudesti e nell'oblio fatto sì grande,
3 Degno d'un chiaro sol, degno d'un pieno
4 Teatro opre sarian sì memorande,
5 Piacciati ch'indi il tragga e'n bel sereno
6 Alle future età lo spieghi e mande
7 Viva la fama lor e tra lor gloria
8 Splenda del fosco tuo l'alta memoria.

Night, you who within your deep dark breast
Conceal in oblivion a feat so great
—Worthy of clear daylight, of a full
Theater, would be events so memorable—
May it please you that I bring it forth and, in the open,
To future ages reveal and proclaim it.
Long live their fame and, in their glory,
Let shine the lofty memory of your darkness!

They neither flinch, nor parry, nor retreat,
Nor does dexterity here play a role.
They do not give blows now feigned,
 now full, now weak;
The darkness and their rage prevent the use
 of strategy.
Hear their swords clashing horribly
In the middle of the blades—and their feet
 remain planted.
Their feet always firm, hands always in
 motion,
No stroke falls in vain, nor any swordpoint
 astray.

Dishonor [when one is struck] spurs anger
 to revenge,
And revenge then renews dishonor;
Thus constantly to wounding and to haste
New stimulation is added, and new wounds.
Closer and closer they mingle, and closer
Grows the fight, so that swords are useless;
They strike with their pommels, roughly
 and cruelly,
They butt each other with their helmets and
 shields.

Three times the knight squeezes the lady
With strong arms, and each time
From that tenacious embrace she frees herself
—The embrace of a fierce enemy, not a
 lover.
They return to the sword, and each stains it
With much blood; exhausted and breathless,
Each finally retreats
And after long struggles breathes.

IV.

1 Non schivar, non parar, non pur ritrarsi
2 Voglion costor nè qui destrezza ha parte.
3 Non danno i colpi hor finti hor pieni
 hor scarsi;
4 Toglie l'ombra e'l furor l'uso dell'arte.

5 Odi le spade orribilmente urtarsi
6 A mezzo il ferro e'l piè d'orma non parte.

7 Sempre il piè fermo e la man sempre
 in moto
8 Nè scende taglio in van nè punta a voto.

V.

1 L'onta irrita lo sdegno alla vendetta

2 E la vendetta poi l'onta rinnova,
3 Onde sempre al ferir, sempre alla fretta
4 Stimol novo s'aggiunge e piaga nova.
5 D'hor in hor più si mesce e più ristretta
6 Si fa la pugna e spada oprar non giova;
7 Dansi coi pomi e infelloniti e crudi,

8 Cozzan con gli elmi insieme e con gli
 scudi.

VI.

1 Tre volte il cavalier la donna stringe
2 Con le robuste braccia ed altre tante,
3 Poi da quei nodi tenaci ella si scinge,
4 Nodi di fier nemico e non d'amante.

5 Tornano al ferro e l'un e l'altro il tinge
6 Di molto sangue, e stanco ed anelante
7 E questi e quegli alfin pur si ritira
8 E dopo lungo faticar respira.

VII.

The one regards the other, the weight of his pale
Body resting on the pommel of his sword.
By now the rays of the last star are languishing
In the first dawn that has risen in the east.
Tancredi sees the greater quantity of blood
Shed by his enemy and that he himself is not so badly hurt;
In this he rejoices and is proud. Oh, our foolish
Mind, that praises every breath of fortune!

VIII.

Wretched man, in what do you rejoice?
How sad
Will be your triumphs, how unhappy your boasting!
Your eyes will pay, if living you remain,
For each drop of that blood with a sea of tears.
Thus, waiting silently, these
Bloody warriors stopped for a while.
Breaking the silence, finally, Tancredi spoke,
So that each might discover the other's name:

IX.

"It is indeed our misfortune to be employing here
Such valor, when silence covers it.
But since an adverse fate denies us
Praise and witnesses worthy of our deed,
I pray you—if in war there is a place for prayers
—To reveal to me your name and station,
So that I may know, whether in defeat or victory,
Whom my death or my life honors."

VII.

1 L'un l'altro guarda e del suo corpo esangue
2 Sul pomo della spada appoggia il peso.
3 Già de l'ultima stella il raggio langue
4 Sul primo albor ch'è in oriente acceso.
5 Vede Tancredi in maggior copia il sangue
6 Del suo nemico e sè non tanto offeso.
7 Ne gode e insuperbisce. O nostra folle
8 Mente ch'ogni aura di fortuna estolle!

VIII.

1 Misero, di che godi? O quanti mesti
2 Fiano i trionfi ed infelice il vanto!
3 Gli occhi tuoi pagheran, s'in vita resti,
4 Di quel sangue ogni stilla un mar di pianto.
5 Così tacendo e rimandando questi
6 Sanguinosi guerrier cessaro alquanto.
7 Ruppe il silenzio alfin Tancredi e disse,
8 Perchè il suo nome l'un l'altro scoprisse:

IX.

1 "Nostra sventura è ben che qui s'impieghi
2 Tanto valor dove silenzio il copra.
3 Ma poi che sorte ria vien che ci nieghi
4 E lode e testimon degni de l'opra,
5 Pregoti, se fra l'armi han loco i prieghi,
6 Che'l tuo nome e'l tuo stato a me tu scopra,
7 Acciò ch'io sappia, o vinto o vincitore,
8 Chi la mia morte o la mia vita honore."

X.

1 Rispose la feroce: "Indarno chiedi	The fierce woman replied: "In vain you ask
2 Quel ch'ho per uso di non far palese,	That which I am not accustomed to reveal,
3 Ma, chiunque io mi sia, tu innanzi vedi	But, whoever I am, you see before you
4 Un di quei duo che la gran torre accese."	One of the two who burned the great tower."[7]
5 Arse di sdegno a quel parlar Tancredi	Burning with rage at this speech, Tancredi
6 E "In mal punto il dicesti," [indi riprese,]	Replied: "It was poorly calculated to say that;
7 "E'l tuo dir e'l tacer di par m'alletta,	Both your speech and your silence equally invite me,
8 Barbaro discortese, alla vendetta."	Ignoble barbarian, to vengeance."

XI.

1 Torna l'ira nei cori e li trasporta	Anger returns to their hearts and carries them,
2 Benche deboli in guerra a fiera pugna	Although weakened by war, to fierce combat,
3 U'l'arte in bando, u'già la forza è morta,	Where skill is abandoned and strength is already dead,
4 Ove invece d'entrami il furor pugna!	Where instead of these things, [only] rage fights.
5 Oh che sanguigna e spaziosa porta	Oh what a bloody and spacious gateway
6 Fa l'una e l'altra spada ovunque giugna	Makes each sword wherever it reaches
7 Nell'armi e nelle carni! e se la vita	Into armor or flesh! And if life
8 Non esce, sdegno tienla al petto unita.	Does not depart, it is because anger holds it united to their breast.

XII.

1 Ma ecco homai l'hora fatal è giunta	But see, now the fatal hour has arrived
2 Che'l viver di Clorinda al suo fin deve.	When the life of Clorinda to its end must come.
3 Spinge egli il ferro nel bel sen di punta	He thrusts the end of his sword into her beautiful breast,
4 Che vi s'immerge e'l sangue avido beve,	So that it immerses itself and eagerly drinks the blood,
5 E la veste che, d'or vago trapunta,	And the garment, with gold beautifully embroidered,

---

[7]Clorinda had been one of two Muslim warriors responsible for burning the siege tower that the Christians had been using in their attack on Jerusalem.

6 That clasps her tender, delicate breasts,
7 Fills with a hot stream. She already feels
8 Herself dying and her feet give out, weak and collapsing.

XIII.
1 He follows up his victory, and the wounded
2 Maiden is menacingly pursued and pressed.
3 She, as she falls, her afflicted voice
4 Moving, speaks her final words,
5 Words spoken to her by a new spirit,
6 A spirit of faith, charity, and hope,
7 Virtues that God instills in her, for though a rebel
8 In life was she, he wishes her in death his servant.

XIV.
1 "Friend, you have won. I pardon you; pardon
2 Me as well—not my body, which fears nothing—
3 But my soul. Pray for it, and give
4 Baptism to me, which all my sins washes."
5 In this dying voice there resounded
6 Something so mournful and soft
7 That it rose to his heart and all anger died,
8 And his eyes to tears were induced and forced.

XV.
1 Nor far from there, in the hollow of the mountain,
2 Gushed murmuring a little stream.
3 He ran to it and filled his helmet in the spring,
4 And returned sadly to his great and pious duty.
5 He felt his hand tremble as the face,
6 As yet unknown, was unmasked and revealed.

6 Le mammelle stringea tenere e lieve,
7 L'empie d'un caldo fiume. Ella già sente
8 Morirsi e'l piè le manca egro e languente.

XIII.
1 Segue egli la vittoria, e la traffitta
2 Vergine minacciando incalza e preme.
3 Ella, mentre cadea, la voce afflitta
4 Movendo, disse le parole estreme,
5 Parole ch'a lei novo spirto ditta,
6 Spirto di fè, di carità, di speme,
7 Virtù che Dio l'infonde, e se rubella
8 In vita fu, la vol in morte ancella.

XIV.
1 "Amico, hai vinto. Io ti perdon, perdona
2 Tu ancora—al corpo no, che nulla pave—
3 All'alma sì. Deh per lei prega e dona
4 Battesmo a me, ch'ogni mia colpa lave."
5 In queste voci languide risuona
6 Un non so che di flebile e soave
7 Ch'al cor gli scende ed ogni sdegno ammorza
8 E gli occhi a lagrimar l'invoglia e sforza.

XV.
1 Poco quindi lontan, ne sen del monte,
2 Scaturia mormorando un picciol rio.
3 Egli v'accorse e l'elmo empiè nel fonte,
4 E tornò mesto al grande ufficio e pio.
5 Tremar sentì la man mentre la fronte
6 Non conosciuta ancor sciolse e scoprio.

7 La vide e la conobbe e restò senza

He saw her and recognized her and was struck

8 E voce e moto. Ahi vista! ahi conoscenza!

Voiceless and motionless. What vision! What revelation!

XVI.

1 Non morì già che sue virtuti accolse

He did not yet die, for gathering his strength

2 Tutte in quel punto e in guardia al cor le mise;

Together in one place, he set it to guard his heart,

3 E premendo il suo affanno a dar si volse

And putting aside his anguish turned to give

4 Vita con l'acqua a chi col ferro uccise.

Life with water to her whom with iron he had killed.

5 Mentre egli il suon de'sacri detti sciolse,

While he unfurled the sound of the sacred words,

6 Colei di gioia trasmutossi e rise,

She, with joy transformed, smiled,

7 E in atto di morir lieta e vivace

And, at the moment of death, happy and full of life,

8 Dir parea: "S'apre il ciel, io vado in pace."

Seemed to say: "Heaven opens; I go in peace."

—Torquato Tasso (*Gerusalemme liberata*, Canto 12, stanzas 52–62 and 64–68)

EDITION

Our edition is, as in Selection 4, an earlier twentieth-century one. Although largely true to the original part books of Monteverdi's Eighth Book of Madrigals, the editor has added indications of dynamics and tempo as well as a realization of the figured bass. Monteverdi's original dynamics are spelled out in italics, as in measures 171–72, where the word *piano* is closely followed by *forte*.[8] Also original are a number of other indications given in regular type, translated below:

m. 18: *motto del cavallo* = "motion of the horse"

m. 73: *sinfonia* = "instrumental passage"

mm. 80 and 106: *passeggio* probably refers to what would later be called a ritornello

m. 174: *qui si lascia l'arco, e si strappano le corde con duoi ditti* = "here the bow is put down and the strings are pulled with two fingers" —that is, a strong pizzicato

m. 183: *qui si ripiglia l'arco* = "here the bow is taken up again"

---

[8]The editor's suggestion to play a crescendo here is surely a correct interpretation of Monteverdi's intention.

mm. 366ff.: *arcata sola* = "in one bow," that is, go from *forte* to *piano* in a single bow

m. 445 (strings): *queste ultima nota va in arcata morendo* = "this last note is bowed [so as to] die away"

m. 445 (Clorinda): *lunga voce in piano* = "long note, becoming soft"

Omitted from this edition is another indication at measure 133: *principio della guerra* = "beginning of the battle."

The archaic triple-time signatures at measure 18 and elsewhere probably imply a specific tempo relationship with the preceding common-time sections. The editor suggests equating each half-measure of this triple time with a quarter note in the preceding section (see m. 38). But this and other editorial tempo equations in the score probably assume too slow a tempo for the common-time sections, whose beat might fall instead on the half note.

In measures 130–32 the tenor partbook contains an embellished version of the line given in our edition:

PERFORMANCE ISSUES

Monteverdi's foreword specifies that the accompanying instruments were to be what we would call a string quartet—two violins, viola, and an instrument resembling the cello—plus a contrabass viola da gamba and harpsichord. Many aspects of violin construction and technique at this date differed from those of modern instruments but can be reconstructed from surviving instruments, pictures, and written accounts. By the same token, the nature of early-Baroque Italian harpsichords is fairly well understood, although the precise manner of realizing the figured bass is more difficult to ascertain. The editorial continuo realization in our edition was intended for the piano and omits the arpeggiation and other ornaments that a harpsichordist of Monteverdi's day would probably have employed. Although the interpretation of the harmony is largely correct, many details of the realization, such as the high register in measures 108–9 and the passing notes in measures 118–23 (in part to reflect changing notes in the voice), are contrary to seventeenth-century practice.

Monteverdi directs that the playing reflect the changing emotional character of the text, implying changes of tempo and dynamics beyond those indicated in the score. Similarly, the narrator is enjoined to sing in a way that reflects the "emotions of the oration" and not to add any embellishments except in Stanza 3, the invocation of Night.

The composer's foreword also describes an early staged performance in which the two characters sang in costume as they acted out the scene; Tancredi even made his entrance on some sort of hobby horse (a *cavallo mariano*)! Presumably this stage machine, as well as the stage action, was stylized rather than realistic; Monteverdi's foreword suggests that the action was choreographed so that the actors moved and struck their blows in time with the music. Today this work is usually performed in concert, without staging, but one wonders how the musical effects might be enhanced by appropriate lighting, scenery, costume, and action.

8. Pier Francesco Cavalli (1602–1676), *Giasone* (opera: selections)

a. Act 1, scene 14 ("Dell'antro magico")

Del la - go sti - gi - o I fo - chi splen - di-no,

E sù ne man - di - no Fu - mi, che tur - bi-no La lu-ce al

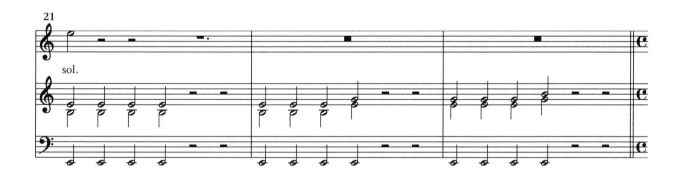

sol.

Dal - l'ab-bru-cia - te gle-be Gran mo-nar - ca del - l'om-bre in-ten - to a - scol - ta-mi,

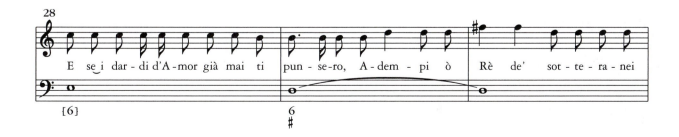

E se i dar - di d'A-mor già mai ti pun-se-ro, A-dem-pi ò Rè de' sot-te-ra-nei

[6]
6
#

Al mio so - glio, Qua, qua vi vo - glio.

A che si tar - da più? Nu - mi Tar - ta - re - i sù, sù, sù, sù!

Coro di spiriti a 4

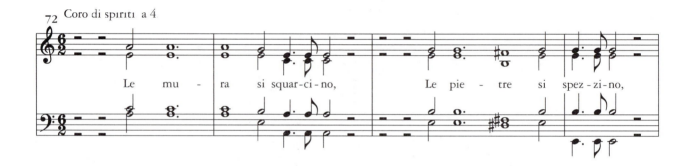

Le mu - ra si squar - ci - no,   Le pie - tre si spez - zi - no,

Le mo - li si fran - ghi - no,   Va - cil - - li - no,

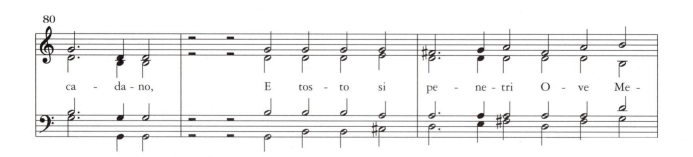

ca - da - no,   E tos - to si pe - ne - tri O - ve Me -

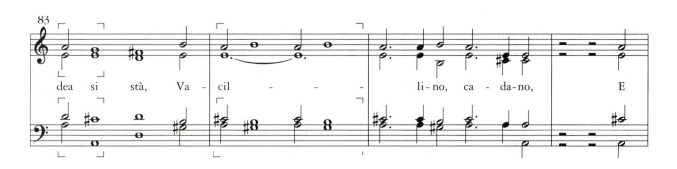

dea si stà, Va - cil - - - li-no, ca - da-no, E

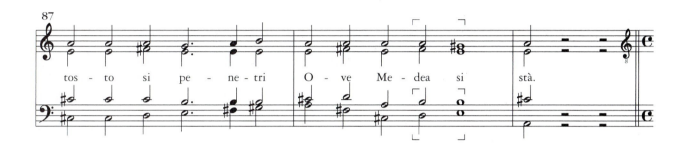

tos - to si pe - ne - tri O - ve Me - dea si stà.

Volano.

Spirito

Del gran du - ce tar - ta - re - o Le tue pre-ci o Me - dea, Gl'ar - bi - tri

le - ga - no E i nu-mi in-fer-ni a cen - ni tuoi si pie - ga-no, Plu - to le tue

vo - ci u - dì. In que - sto cer - chio d'or Si ra-chiu - d'il va -

[4   #]

lor. Che di Gia-son il cor Ar-me-rà que-sto dì.

Medea.

Si, si, si, Vin-ce-rà Il mio re, Si, si, si, Vin-ce rà, vin-ce-

rà il mio re, Al suo pro De-i-tà Di la giù Pu-gne-

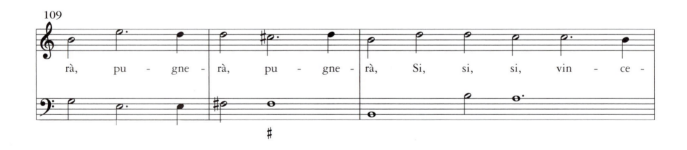

rà, pu-gne-rà, pu-gne-rà, Si, si, si, vin-ce-

rà, vin-ce-rà, si, si, si, vin-ce-rà, vin-ce-rà.

b. Act 3, scene 21 ("Infelice ch'ascolto?")

TEXT AND TRANSLATION

Medea

Dell antro magico,
Stridenti cardini,
Il varco apritemi,
E frà le tenebre
Del negro ospitio
Lassate me.
Su l'ara orribile
Del lago stigio
I fochi splendino,
E sù ne mandino
Fumi, che turbino
La luce al sol.
Dall'abbruciate glebe,
Gran monarca dell'ombre intento
  ascoltami,
E se i dardi d'Amor già mai ti punsero,
Adempi, ò Rè de' sotterranei popoli,
L'amoroso desio che'l cor mi stimola,
E tutto Averno alla bell'opra uniscasi.
I mostri formidabili,
Del bel vello di Frisso
Sentinelle feroci infaticabili,
Per potenza d'abisso
Si rendono a Giasone oggi domabili.
Dall'arsa Dite
(Quante portate
Serpi alla fronte),
Furie, venite,
E di Pluto gl'imperi a me svelate.
Già percoto
Il suol col piè:
Orridi
Demoni,
Spiriti
D'Erebo,
Volate a me.
Così indarno vi chiamo?
Quai strepiti,
Quai sibili,
Non lascian penetrar nel cieco baratro
Le mie voci terribili?
Dalla sabbia
Di Cocito

Tutta rabbia
Quà v'invito
Al mio soglio,
Quà, vi voglio;
A che si tarda più?

Medea

Creaking hinges,
Open for me the door
Of the magical cave,
And in the darkness
Of the black shelter
Let me in.
Above the horrible altar
Of the Stygian lake[9]
The flames sparkle
And send up
Smoke that clouds
The light of the sun.
From your singed rocks,
Great monarch of the shades, hear me
  carefully,
And if the arrows of Love ever wounded you,
Fulfill, king of the underworld peoples,
The amorous desire that urges my heart
And let all Avernus join in the fair work.
Formidable monsters,
Fierce, tireless sentinels
Of Phrixos's beautiful fleece,
By the power of the abyss
Let you be tamed today by Jason.
From burning Dis [Hades]
—How many serpents
You carry on your face!—
Furies, come,
And show me the domain of Pluto.
Already the earth
Shakes at my feet.
Horrid
Demons,
Spirits
Of Erebus,
Fly to me!
In vain do I call you?
What noises,
What hissing
Prevent my terrible words from
Penetrating the blind abyss?
From the sands
Of Cocytus [another lake of the
  Underworld],
Enraged
I summon you
To my throne;
I demand you—
Why do you delay?

---

[9]In Classical mythology, the Styx was one of the rivers (here, a lake) of the underworld.

Coro	**Chorus**
Le mura si squarcino,	Let the walls [of the city] be torn down,
Le pietre si spezzino,	Let the building stones be smashed,
Le moli si franghino,	Let the structures be broken.
Vacillino, cadano	Let them shake and fall
E tosto si penetri	And soon be pierced
Ove Medea si stà.	Where Medea wishes.
Volano.	*They fly.*
Spirito	**A spirit**
Del gran duce tartareo	The great leader of the underworld
Le tue preci, o Medea,	Is bound, O Medea
Gl'arbitrii legano	By your will,
Ei numi inferni ai cenni tuoi si piegano,	And the infernal spirits yield to your command.
Pluto le tue voci udì.	Pluto has heard your voice.
	{Handing her a large magic ring}
In questo cerchio d'or	This golden ring
Si racchiude valor,	Possesses power
Che di Giasone il cor	That today will arm
Armerà questo dì.	Jason's heart.
Medea	**Medea**
Si, si, si,	Yes, yes, yes,
Vincerà	He will win,
Il mio rè.	My king.
Al suo prò	For him
Deità	The god
Di la giù	Of below
Pugnerà.	Will fight.
Si, si, si,	Yes, yes, yes,
Vincerà.	He will win.
. . .	. . .
Isifile	**Hypsipyle**
Infelice, che ascolto?	Unfortunate me, whom do I hear?
Non t'affannar, Giasone,	Do not worry, Jason,
Che, se la vita mia	For, if my life
Fu (come ben intesi)	Has been (as I well have understood)
Un aborto d'errori	A monstrosity of errors
Che produce il tuo duolo,	Producing your grief,
Vengo a sacrificarla a'tuoi furori.	I come to sacrifice it to your anger.
S'io perivo tra l'acque,	Had I perished in the water,
Una morte sì breve	A death so quick
Forse non appagava i tuoi rigori.	Might not have satisfied your harshness.
Ma, se viva son io,	But, since I am alive,
Rallegrati, o crudele,	Be glad, cruel one,
Già che potrai con replicate morti	For you can, through repeated deaths,
Sfogar nel fiero cor l'empio desio.	Satisfy in your fierce heart your wicked desire.
Sì, sì, tiranno mio,	Yes, yes, my tyrant,
Ferisci a parte a parte	Dismember into pieces
Queste membra aborrite,	These hated limbs,
Sbranami a poco a poco	Tear, little by little,
Queste carni infelici,	This unfortunate flesh,
Anatomizza il seno,	Dissect my breast,

Straziami a tuo piacere,
Martirizami i sensi,
E'l mio lento morire
Prolunghi a me'l tormento, a te'l gioire.
Ma se d'esser marito
L'adorate memorie alfin perdesti,
Fa ch'il nome di padre
Fra le tue crudeltadi intatto resti.
Non ti scordar, Giason, che padre sei,
E che son di te parte i parti miei.
Se legge di natura
Obliga agl'alimenti anco le fiere,
Fa che mano pietosa
Gli sominstri almen vitto mendico,
E non soffrir ch'i tuoi scettrati figli
Per la fame languenti
Spirin l'alme innocenti.
Regina, Egeo, amici,
Supplicate per me questo crudele,
Ch nel ferir mi lasci
Queste mammelle da'suoi colpi intatte,
Acciò nutrisca almen i figli miei
Dal morto sen materno un freddo latte.
Pregatelo pietosi
Che quegl'angeli infanti
Assistino ai martiri
Della madre tradita,
E ch'ad ogni ferita
Ch'imprimerà nel mio pudico petto
Bevino quelli il sangue mio stillante,
Acciò ch'ei, trapassando
Nelle lor pure vene, in lor s'incarni,
Ond'il lor seno in qualche parte sia
Tomba innocente, all'innocenza mia.
Addio terra, addio sole,
Addio regina amica, amici, addio;
Addio scettri, addio patria, addio mia
  prole.
Scolta la madre vostra
Dal suo terrestre velo
Attenderà di rivedervi in cielo.
Venite, cari pegni,
Temp'è che vi consegni
All'adorato mostro,
Ch'è carnefice mio, e padre vostro.
Figli, v'attendo e moro,
E te, Giason, benchè omicida, adoro.

—Giacinto Andrea Cicognini

Destroy me to your pleasure,
Torment my senses,
And prolong my slow death
To my torment and your enjoyment.
But if you already have lost
The adored memory of being a husband,
Let the name of "father"
Remain untouched by your cruelties.
Do not forget, Jason, that you are a father,
And that your children are also mine.
If a law of nature
Makes even wild animals feed them,[10]
Let your pitying hand
Give them at least a beggar's diet
And let not your sceptered sons,
Weak from hunger,
Give up their innocent souls.
Queen [Medea], [King] Aegeus, friends,
Plead for me with this cruel one
That in striking me he leave
My breasts untouched by his blows,
So that at least my sons may be nourished
By cold milk from a dead maternal breast.
Beg of him pitiably
That these angelic children
Be present at the martyrdom
Of their betrayed mother,
And that with every wound
That strikes my chaste breast
They may drink my dripping blood,
Which, passing
Into their pure veins, will become theirs,
And their breasts will in some part be
An innocent tomb for my innocence.
Farewell, earth; farewell, sun;
Farewell, queen, my friend; friends, farewell;
Farewell, scepter; farewell, country; farewell,
  my children.
Your mother, released
From her earthly form
Will look forward to seeing you in heaven.
Come, dear children,
It is time that I consign you
To the beloved monster
Who is my killer and your father.
Children, I keep you and I die,
And you, Jason, though a murderer, I adore.

---

[10]This might refer to the Roman myth of Remus and Romulus, who as infants were nourished by a she-wolf.

EDITION

Our edition reflects the surviving manuscript scores of the work. The barlines are placed irregularly, following a characteristic source (see below).

PERFORMANCE ISSUES

Unlike the printed score of *Orfeo*, the manuscripts of *Giasone* provide few details of performance. Although the precise instrumentation must have varied, most performances were probably scored quite economically, using an ensemble similar to that of Monteverdi's *Combattimento*: a few bowed strings and a small continuo group. Good acting and stagecraft, rather than overblown orchestration, must have been important to the work's effect, alongside singing that employed a certain amount of rhythmic freedom and virtuoso embellishment but was above all always sensitive to Cavalli's musical rhetoric.

SOURCE

The present edition has been prepared after consultation with the manuscript Venice, Biblioteca Nazionale Marciana, IV, 363 (9887).

9. Barbara Strozzi (1619–1677), *Ardo in tacito foco* (cantata or strophic aria)

TEXT AND TRANSLATION

Cuore che reprime alla lingua di manifestare il nome della sua cara

A heart that prevents the tongue from revealing the name of its beloved

Prima parte

Stanza 1

1 Ardo in tacito foco,
2 Neppure m'è concesso
3 Dal geloso cor mio
4 Far palese a me stesso
5 Il nome di colei ch'è 'l mio desio
6 Ma nel carcer del seno
7 Racchiuso tien l'ardore
8 Carcerier di se stesso, il proprio core,
9 E appena sia contento
10 Con aliti e sospiri
11 Far palese a la lingua i suoi martiri.

I burn in silent fire,
For I am even prevented
By my own jealous heart
From revealing to myself
The name of her who is my desire.
But in the prison of my breast
My ardor holds bound
My own heart as its prisoner,
And it is barely content
Through breaths and sighs
To reveal to the tongue its suffering.

Seconda parte

Stanza 2

12 Se pur, per mio ristoro,
13 Con tributi di pianto
14 Mostrar voglio con fede
15 A quella ch'amo tanto
16 Che son d'Amor le lagrime mercede,
17 Ecco'l cor, ch'esalando
18 Di più sospiri il vento
19 Assorbe il pianto e quel umor n'ha spento.
20 E con mio duol m'addita
21 Che gl'occhi lagrimanti
22 Sono muto le lingue ne gl'amanti.

Even if, for my consolation,
Through payments in tears
I were to show, in truth,
To her whom I love so much,
That tears are the payment for [my] love,
Then, as the heart exhaled
Even more sighs, the wind would
Soak up the tears and the latter would be all spent.
And, to my grief, it shows
That weeping eyes
Are the silent tongues of lovers.

Terza & ultima parte

Stanza 3

23 Qual sia l'aspro mio stato
24 Ridir nol ponno i venti,
25 Ne pur le selve o l'onde
26 Udiro i miei lamenti,
27 Ma solo il duol entro al mio cor s'asconde.
28 E quale in chiuso specco
29 Disfassi pietra al foco
30 Tal'io m'incenerisco a poco a poco,
31 E s'ad'altri la lingua
32 È scorta alla lor sorte
33 A me la lingua è sol cagion di morte.

How bitter my state is
Cannot be recounted by the winds,
Nor have the woods or the waves
Heard my complaints;
Only sadness hides itself within my heart.

And as beneath a concave mirror
A stone melts in the fire,
So am I reduced to ashes, little by little,
And if for others the tongue
Guides them to their fortune,
To me the tongue is only the cause of death.

—Giovanni Francesco Loredano (?)

EDITION

The original notation, which can be seen in Figures 5.1 of the text volume, has been modernized: barlines have been regularized and note values in the triple-time sections are half those of the original.

PERFORMANCE ISSUES

In theory, the changing time signatures at this date still indicated proportional tempo relationships; presumably a whole note in the common-time sections was understood to have the same duration as a dotted whole note in triple time (as notated here). But the vocal part no doubt was performed with considerable dynamic contrast and freedom of tempo and rhythm, reflecting the words. This would have been especially true of the sections in common time; the triple-time sections should probably flow more smoothly. The tempo marks *adagio* and *presto* probably signify relatively small differences in speed, less than the words do today; despite the notation in large note values, even the *adagio* sections should probably be "in one," the beat falling on the dotted whole note.

The precise meaning of the slurs is uncertain and may vary from one instance to another. Some slurs may have served merely to indicate that two notes were to be sung to the same syllable (see m. 13 as it appears in Fig. 5.1 in the text volume). Others call attention to special motivic figures, as on the chromatic line in measures 91–93 (printed in the original as a series of two-note slurs) and on many two-note figures spanning a half step, as in measures 29–30, where the slur on the syllable *-o* marks what was known as *anticipazione della syllaba*. In such cases the slur may be a signal for particularly expressive performance, perhaps including vibrato or tremolo on the first note. In measure 9 the slur beginning on a tied note might similarly imply a swell (*messa di voce*) that peaks on the first note of the slur.

Strozzi provides virtually no clues to the realization of the continuo part (there are only a few figures, as in m. 32). Whether played on a form of lute or harpsichord, the realization should surely be simple, never distracting attention from the voice. Historical use of more than a single continuo instrument in a work such as this is unlikely.

SOURCE

This edition has been newly prepared from a facsimile of the first edition.[11]

---

[11]*Cantate ariete à una, due, e tre voci*, op. 3 (Venice, 1654); for the facsimile of the original edition, see the bibliography in the text volume.

10. Alessandro Scarlatti (1660–1725), *Correa nel seno amato* (cantata: selections)

a. Aria "Fresche brine"

Fre — sche bri — ne che pie — to — se,

*Second time: end here, then repeat measures 1–20.

b. Aria "Onde belle"

On - de bel -

on - de bel - - le, che pie - to - -

se   que - sti pra - ti   rin   fre - sca - - - -

♭6   ♭7 6   ♯6
              4

- - te,   a - scol - ta - -

6   6 ♯6

— — — — — te,

e do-lo-ro — se, e do-lo-ro —

se con lu-gu — bre mor — mo — ri — o, con lu-gu — bre

TEXT AND TRANSLATION

1	Fresche brine che pietose	Fresh frost so merciful,	
2	Ravvivate queste rose	Revive these roses	
3	E baciate il lembo ai fior,	And kiss the tips of the flowers.	
4	Deh, cadete e pallidette,	Ah, fallen and pale,	
5	Trasformate in lagrimette,	Transformed into little tears	
6	Sol piangete al mio dolor.	You weep alone at my sorrow.	

. . .   . . .

1	Onde belle, che pietose	Waves, lovely and merciful,
2	Questi prati rinfrescate,	Who refresh these meadows,
3	Ascoltate, e dolorose,	Listen [to me], and, saddened,
4	Con lugubre mormorio,	With lugubrious murmurings,
5	Deh, piangete al pianto mio.	Ah, weep with my weeping.

PERFORMANCE ISSUES

The manuscript scores preserving Scarlatti's cantatas leave open the questions of what type of voice—female or male castrato—sang them and whether the violin parts were played by soloists or multiple players. The instrumentation of the continuo part is likewise left open, although by this date both harpsichord and cello are likely to have participated (Scarlatti was himself a keyboard player, and two other movements of this cantata are exceptional in including short passages in which the right-hand part is written out for the harpsichordist). No doubt the singer was expected to add a certain amount of improvised ornamentation, but the elaborate decoration of da capo arias that would become standard practice in the eighteenth century was probably not yet a regular feature and would seem inappropriate to the relatively simple style of "Fresche brine."

SOURCE

The cantata is preserved in several eighteenth-century manuscripts. For a realization of the continuo part, see the modern edition of the complete work.[12]

---

[12]Alessandro Scarlatti, *Correa nel seno amato*, ed. Otto Drechsler (Kassel, Germany: Bärenreiter, 1974).

11. Henry Purcell (1659–95), *From Rosy Bowers* (cantata)

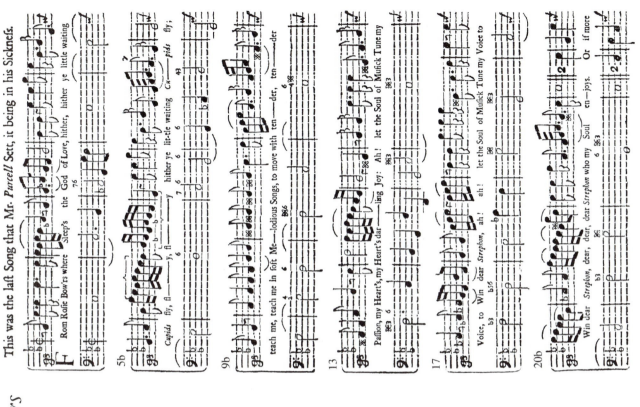

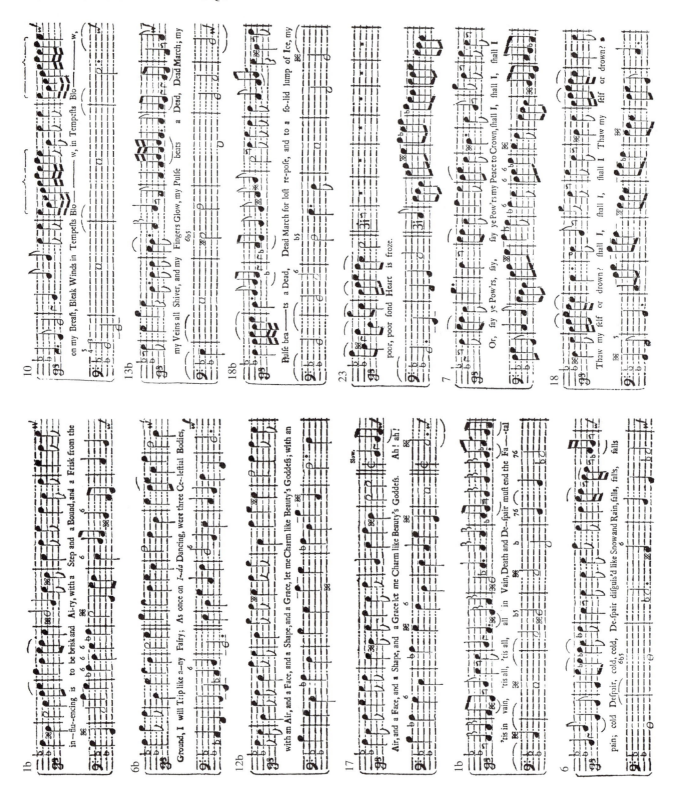

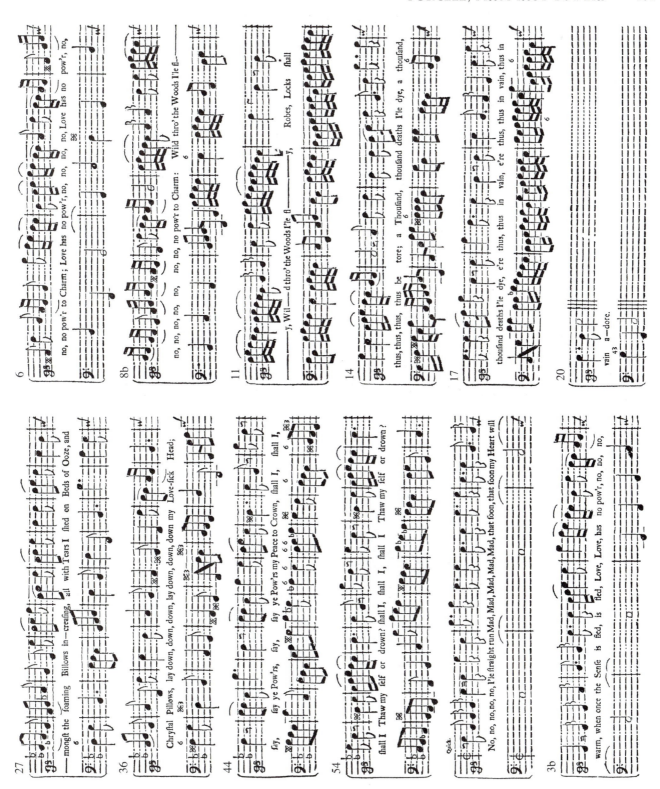

TEXT

[*I. Recitative*]

1 From rosy bowers where sleeps the god of love,
2 Hither, ye little waiting Cupids, fly;
3 Teach me in soft melodious songs to move
4 With tender passion my heart's darling joy:
5 Ah! let the soul of music tune my voice,
6 To win dear Strephon,* who my soul enjoys.

*Don Quixote

[*II. Air*]

1 Or if more influencing
2 Is to be brisk and airy,
3 With a step and a bound
4 And a frisk* from the ground
5 I will trip* like any fairy;
6 As once on Ida* dancing
7 Were three celestial bodies,*
8 With an air, and a face,
9 And a shape, and a grace,
10 Let me charm like beauty's goddess.*

*a playful leap (?)
*dance lightly
*mountain near ancient Troy
*the Graces, minor female deities

*Venus

[*III. Recitative*]

1 Ah! 'tis in vain, 'tis all, 'tis all in vain,
2 Death and despair must end the fatal pain;
3 Cold despair, disguis'd like snow and rain,
4 Falls on my breast; bleak winds in tempests blow,
5 My veins all shiver, and my fingers glow;
6 My pulse beats a dead march* for lost repose,
7 And to a solid lump of ice my poor fond heart is
   froze.

*funeral march

[*IV. Air*]

1 Or say, ye powers, my peace to crown,
2 Shall I thaw myself or drown?
3 Amongst the foaming billows,
4 Increasing all with tears I shed,
5 On beds of ooze, and crystal pillows,
6 Lay down, lay down my lovesick head.

[*V. Recitative*]

1 No, no, I'll straight run mad,
2 That soon my heart will warm;
3 When once the sense is fled,
4 Love has no power to charm.
5   Wild through the woods I'll fly;
6   Robes, locks shall thus be tore.
7   A thousand deaths I'll die
8   Ere* thus in vain adore.   *before

—Thomas D'Urfey

EDITION

Our edition is a facsimile from an early printed collection of Purcell's songs in which it bears the heading "The last song the author set, it being in his sickness." This claim that Purcell wrote the music while suffering from his final illness has not been confirmed.

The notation is essentially that used today except for a few readily understood differences. For example, the clefs at the opening have a slightly different appearance from their modern counterparts, but they are the treble G clef and bass F clef of today. The little squiggle at the end of each line is a *custos* that points to the next pitch at the beginning of the following line or page. There are also some differences in the use of accidentals. Some flats are placed under, rather than in front of, the notes to which they apply (as in m. 6). What we would call the sharp sign is used to indicate B natural (as in m. 11).

The time signature "2" used for the second section ("Or if more influencing") probably stands for a quick form of duple time (modern $\frac{2}{2}$). In the fourth section, the time signature "3 1" is equivalent to modern $\frac{3}{8}$; it too probably implies a relatively quick tempo.[13]

At measure 4 of the third section, another early printed source gives an alternate version, accentuating the word *death* through the unusual upward leap of a diminished octave:

---

[13]For an edition in modern notation, see *The Works of Henry Purcell*, vol. 16, *Dramatic Music: Part 1*, edited by the Purcell Society (London: Novello, 1906), 181–93; a revised edition was announced for publication in 2007.

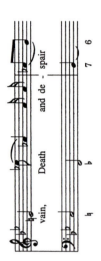

PERFORMANCE ISSUES

This composition was written as a musical scene for a larger theatrical work, Part 3 of an English adaptation of Cervantes's *Don Quixote*. But its publication as a self-contained "song" within a few years of Purcell's death shows that, like most of Purcell's stage music, it was also performed on its own, often no doubt by amateurs in domestic settings. The two parts are unlabeled, but the upper is certainly for a female soprano, the lower a continuo part that would have been realized by harpsichord with an optional viola da gamba or cello doubling the bass line.[14]

Only the third and the fifth sections bear tempo marks—in English, suggesting that Purcell's readers were as yet unfamiliar with what are now commonly understood Italian tempo words. Some of the original "time signatures" have implications for tempo as well. There is a single ornament sign, in measure 8 of the opening section (probably a trill), but performers would have added numerous ornaments elsewhere, particularly at cadences.

The double bar in the middle of the second section is probably an indication that at least the first half of this section is to be repeated.

SOURCES

Our facsimile is from *Orpheus Britannicus* (The British Orpheus; London, 1698; 2nd. ed., 1721).[15] The alternate reading shown above is from *New Songs in the Third Part of the Comical History of Don Quixote Written by Mr. Durfey* (London, 1696).[16]

---

[14]For a realization of the continuo part, see the modern edition mentioned in the previous note.
[15]For the complete two-volume work, see the facsimile published by Broude (New York, 1965). A later edition (London, 1721) has also appeared in facsimile (Ridgewood, N.J.: Gregg Press, 1965).
[16]Facsimile in *Don Quixote: The Music in the Three Plays of Thomas Durfey*, ed. Curtis Price, Music for London Entertainment 1660–1800, ser. A, vol. 2 (Tunbridge Wells, U.K.: Richard MacNutt, 1984), 14–15.

12. Jean-Baptiste Lully (1632–1687), *Armide* (opera: selections)

a. Overture

b. Act 2, scene 5 (recitative "Enfin, il est en ma puissance" and air "Venez seconder mes désirs")

[Armide va pour frapper Renaud et ne ne peut exécuter le dessein qu'elle a de lui ôter la vie.]

TEXT AND TRANSLATION

Armide, *tenant un dard à la main*

Enfin il est en ma puissance,
Ce fatal ennemi, ce superbe vanqueur.
La charme du sommeil le livre à ma
    vengeance;
Je vais percer son invincible coeur.
Par lui, tous mes captifs sont sortis
    d'esclavage;
Qu'il éprouve toute ma rage.
Armide va pour frapper Renaud et ne peut
exécuter le dessein qu'elle a de lui ôter
la vie.
Quel trouble me saisit? qui me fait
    hésiter?
Qu'est-ce qu'en sa faveur la pitié me
    veut dire?
Frappons . . . Ciel! qui peut m'arrêter?

Achevons . . . je frémis! Vengeons-
    nous . . . je soupire!
Est-ce ainsi que je dois me venger
    aujourd'hui?
Ma colère s'éteint quand j'approche
    de lui.
Plus je le vois; plus ma vengeance
    est vaine;
Mon bras tremblant se refuse à ma
    haine.
Ah! quelle cruauté de lui ravir le jour!

A ce jeune héros tout cède sur la terre.

Qui croirait qu'il fût né seulement
    pour la guerre?
Il semble être fait pour l'amour.
Ne puis-je me venger à moins qu'il
    ne périsse?
Hé! ne suffit-il pas que l'Amour le
    punisse?
Puisqu'il n'a pu trouver mes yeux
    assez charmants,
Qu'il m'aime au moins par mes
    enchantements,
Que, s'il se peut, je le haisse.
{Air}
Venez, secondez mes désirs,
Démons, transformez-vous en
    d'aimables zéphirs.
Je cède à ce vainqueur, la pitié me
    surmonte;
Cachez ma faiblesse et ma honte
Dans les plus reculés déserts;
Volez, conduisez-nous au bout de
    l'univers.

—Philippe Quinault

Armide, *holding a dart in her hand*

At last he is in my power,
This fatal enemy, this proud conqueror.
The charm of sleep surrenders him to my
    vengeance;
I shall pierce his invincible heart.
By him were all my captives freed from
    slavery;
Let him feel all my rage.
Armide goes to strike Renaud but is unable to
execute her plan of depriving him of his life.

What disturbance seizes me? what makes
    me hesitate?
What, in his [Renaud's] favor, can pity say
    to me?
[Let me] strike [Renaud] . . . Heavens! what
    could be stopping me?
Let us finish it . . . I tremble! Let us take
    revenge . . . I sigh!
Is this then how I must avenge myself today?

My anger weakens when I approach him.

The more I see him, the more vegeance is
    impossible;
My trembling arm ignores my hate.

Ah, what cruelty it would be to steal
    his life!
To this young hero everything yields
    on earth.
Who would believe he was born only for war?

He seems to be made for love.
Can I be avenged only if he perishes?

Yes, is it not enough that Love punishes him?

Since he could not find my eyes sufficiently
    charming,
Let him at least love me by my
    enchantments,
So that, if it is possible, I shall hate him.
Air
Come, do as I wish,
Demons, transform yourselves into
    pleasant breezes.
I surrender to this conqueror, pity overcomes
    me;
Hide my weakness and my disgrace
In the most faraway deserts;
Fly, lead us to the ends of the world.

EDITION

The score has been newly prepared from early printed sources (see below). In the overture, the instrument names are those traditionally used for the five-part ensemble of French opera; the *dessus* was actually a body of violins, the *haute-contre, taille,* and *quinte de violon* all (probably) taken by violas, while bass violins furnished the bottom part (originally without any continuo realization). The recitative (Selection 12b) immediately follows an orchestral introduction in dotted-overture style that is not reproduced here.

PERFORMANCE ISSUES

French Baroque instrumentation, rhythm, ornamentation, and other aspects of performance involve conventions developed, in part, under Lully's direction. These issues are discussed at length in Chapter 6 of the text volume.

Although continuo instruments were apparently absent from Lully's performances of the overture, the recitative and air for the soprano role of Armide were certainly meant to be accompanied by a realized continuo part, played by harpsichord (or perhaps theorbo), possibly with viola da gamba doubling the bass line. The changing time signatures of the overture and recitative are believed in principle to have had a strict proportional significance, a holdover from Renaissance notation. But sources give conflicting explanations of these time signatures, whose meaning evidently changed or became ambiguous with time. It appears that the quarter note remains constant through all changes of meter, except in measures written in "2" or ¢ Then the beat shifts to the half note, which is equal in value to the quarter note of the surrounding measures.[17] The signature "2" differs from ¢ in that the latter tends to have four quick beats in each measure, whereas the former moves in halfnotes, possibly somewhat slower than those of ¢.

SOURCES

The chief source for our score is the first edition, *Armide, tragédie mise en musique par Monsieur de Lully* (Paris: Ballard, 1686). This has been compared with a reduced (vocal) score published as the *seconde édition* (Paris: Ballard, 1713; fascimile, Beziers: Société de Musicologie de Languedoc [1980].

---

[17]Some uses of ¢ may have been intended simply to allow the equivalent of a half measure of common time (as in m. 35 of the recitative). Today we would use a measure of $\frac{2}{4}$ for this purpose, but such a signature was not yet in use.

13. Giovanni Gabrieli (ca. 1554/7–1612), *In ecclesiis* (*concertato* motet)

TEXT AND TRANSLATION

1	In ecclesiis benedicite Domino.	In the churches, bless the Lord.
2	Alleluia.	Hallelujah.
3	In omni loco dominationis benedic anima mea Dominum.	In every place of [his] power bless, my soul, the Lord.
4	Alleluia.	Hallelujah.
5	In Deo salutari meo et gloria mea,	In God [is] my salvation and my glory,
6	Deus auxilium meum et spes mea in Deo est.	God [is] my help and my hope is in God.
7	Alleluia.	Hallelujah.
8	Deus noster te invocamus, te laudamus, te adoramus.	Our God, we invoke you, we praise you, we praise you, we adore you.
9	Libera nos, salva nos, vivifica nos.	Free us, save us, give us life.
10	Alleluia.	Hallelujah.
11	Deus adjutor noster in aeternum.	God is our hope forever.
12	Alleluia.	Hallelujah.

EDITION

The individual performing parts that comprised the original edition bear traditional Latin headings inherited from the sixteenth century (*cantus, altus, quintus,* etc.). In addition, each is also assigned to a solo vocal part (*voce*), a member of the *capella*, or a specific instrument. The present edition gathers the fourteen main parts into three groups, or choirs; at the top are the solo voices, and at the bottom is a *bassus pro organo* ("bass for the organ"), which today would be called a basso continuo part. To make it easier to take in all fifteen parts at a glance, the present score groups the instrumental and *capella* parts two to a staff. The edition underlays the text only in the *voce* parts and beneath the bass of the *capella* parts, although all four of the latter contain text in the original and were meant to be sung. Note values in the triple-meter sections have been reduced by one half.

The three cornettos include two sopranos and an alto; the two trombones (or sackbuts) also fall within distinct tenor and bass ranges, respectively. The part labeled *violino* is actually for what we would call a viola, as the range and the clef in the original edition would have made clear.

PERFORMANCE ISSUES

There is no indication that the four *capella* parts should be doubled (either by instruments or by multiple voices), nor is there any reason to think that Gabrieli expected a theorbo, violone, or other string instrument to join the organ. Although such doublings are common today and cannot be ruled out as historical practices, this work can be satisfactorily performed by fifteen musicians.

The highest vocal parts originally may have been performed by male castratos. Although boys or falsetto voices might also have been used, women's voices would not have been heard in a Venetian church of the period. The four solo parts were probably sung with a certain amount of improvised embellishment, possibly including some of the ornaments described in Caccini's *Nuove musiche*.

It is believed that in performances at St. Mark's, Venice, the various choirs were placed in spatially separated locations at the front of the church, between the altar and the congregation: the *capella* sang from a large pulpit in front of and to one side of the choir screen (*iconostasis*), and the soloists and instruments (including the organ) were heard from two organ lofts, one on either side above and behind the *capella*. The *maestro di capella* presumably stood with the *capella*, beating time for the group as a whole, with another musician in each of the other choirs watching him and beating time for his own group.

There are no tempo indications as such, but, as in works by Monteverdi, Lully, and others, what we would call time signatures are also indications for proportional tempo relationships; that is, a whole note in the sections in duple (or quadruple) meter has the same duration as a dotted whole note in the tripple-time sections. Despite the large note values, the basic tempo remains relatively brisk, as in sixteenth-century polyphony.

SOURCE

The original edition, Giovanni Gabrieli, *Symphoniae sacrae, Liber secundus . . . tam vocibus, quam instrumentis* (Venice: Magni, 1615) has been consulted in microfilm.

14. Heinrich Schütz (1585–1672), *Herr, neige deine Himmel,* SWV 361 (*concertato* motet)

TEXT AND TRANSLATION

1 Herr, neige deine Himmel und fahr herab;	Lord, bow thy heavens and come down,
2 Taste die Berge an, so rauchen sie,	Touch the mountains so that they smoke.
3 Lass blitzen und zerstreuen sie;	Send forth lightning and scatter them;
4 Wirf deine Strahlen und schrecke sie.	Shoot your arrows and destroy them.
5 Sende deine Hand aus der Höhe	Send your hand from the heights
6 Und erlöse mich von grossen Wassern,	And save me from great waters,
7 Und errette mich von der Hand der fremden Kinder.	And preserve me from the hand of foreign peoples.
8 Gott, ich will dir ein neues Lied singen,	God, I will sing you a new song,
9 Ich will dir spielen auf dem Psalter von zehen Saiten.	I will play to you on a psaltery with ten strings.

—Psalm 144:5–7, 9

PERFORMANCE ISSUES

Unlike his teacher Gabrieli, Schütz specified the addition of a bowed string instrument to the continuo part: a "violone," probably signifying a large bass viola da gamba of some type (not a double bass). Although both the violins and the voices might add occasional trills and other ornaments, there is little opportunity for the more elaborate types of improvised embellishment described in contemporary treatises, for Schütz has written out all the necessary melodic figuration. The relatively plain style and the rather sparse original figures of the continuo part imply a simple chordal realization.

As in the previous work, the time signatures also signify tempo proportions. Thus the whole note in the opening section is worth three whole notes in the triple-time section that begins at measure 43.

SOURCES

The score is reproduced from Heinrich Schütz, *Symphoniae sacrae: Zweiter Theil*, ed. Philipp Spitta, *Sämmtliche Werke* 7 (Leipzig: Breitkopf und Härtel, 1888), 127–33.[18] This edition is based closely on the work's original printed source, Schütz's *Symphonarum sacrarum secunda pars, opus 10* (Sacred symphonies, part 2, Dresden, 1647).

---

[18]For a more recent edition including a basso continuo realization, unfortunately transposed to the key of E minor, see Heinrich Schütz, *Symphoniae sacrae II 1647 Nr. 13–22*, ed. Werner Bittinger, *Neue Ausgabe sämtlicher Werke* 16 (Kassel, Germany: Bärenreiter, 1965), 83–92.

15. Heinrich Schütz (1585–1672), *Saul, Saul, was verfolgst du mich?*, SWV 415 (concertato motet)

133

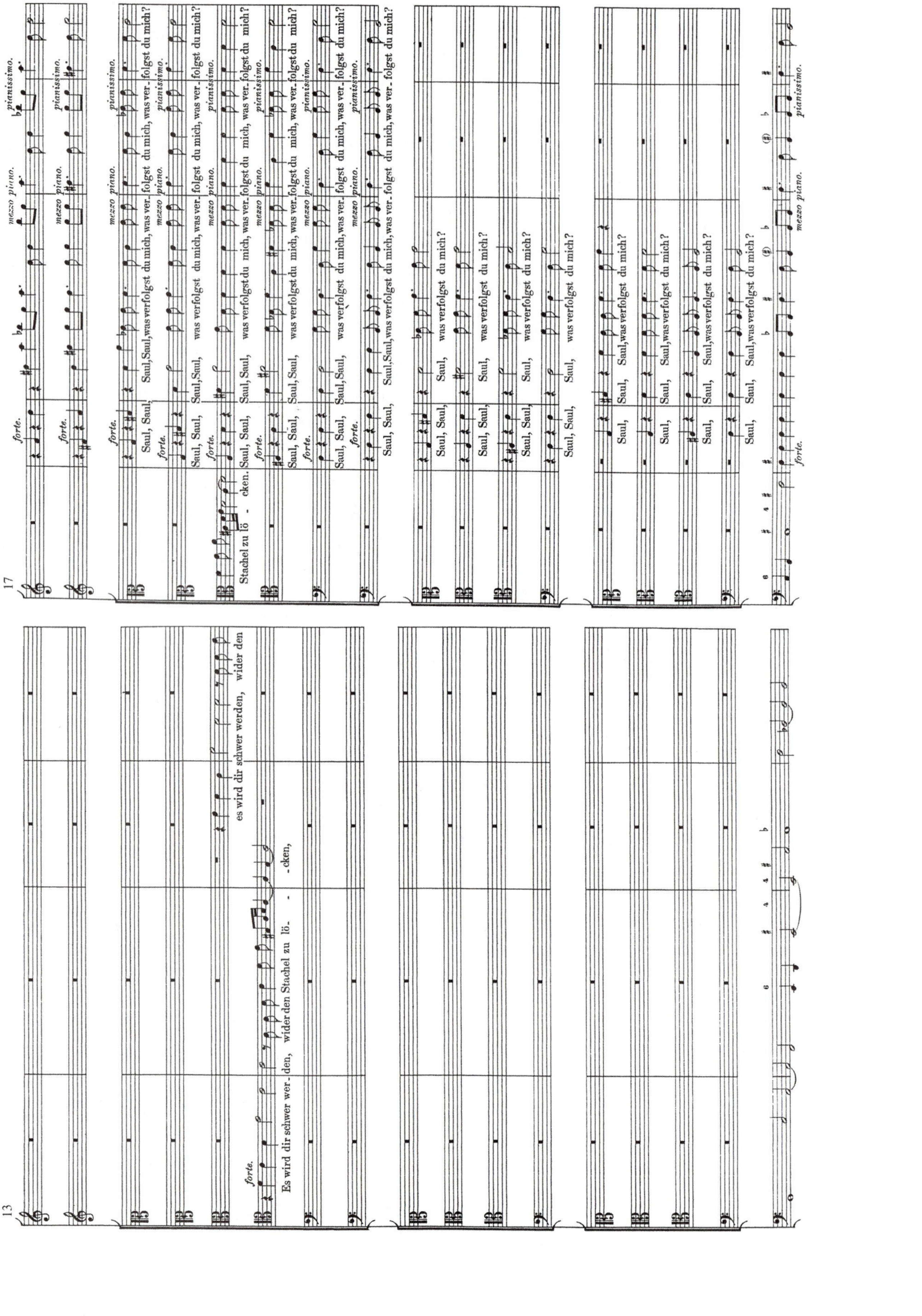
13
17
forte.
Es wird dir schwer wer - den, wider den Stachel zu lö - - cken,
es wird dir schwer werden, wider den Stachel zu lö - cken.
Saul, Saul, Saul, Saul, was verfolgst du mich, was ver - folgst du mich, was ver - folgst du mich?
Saul, Saul, Saul, was verfolgst du mich?
mezzo piano.
pianissimo.

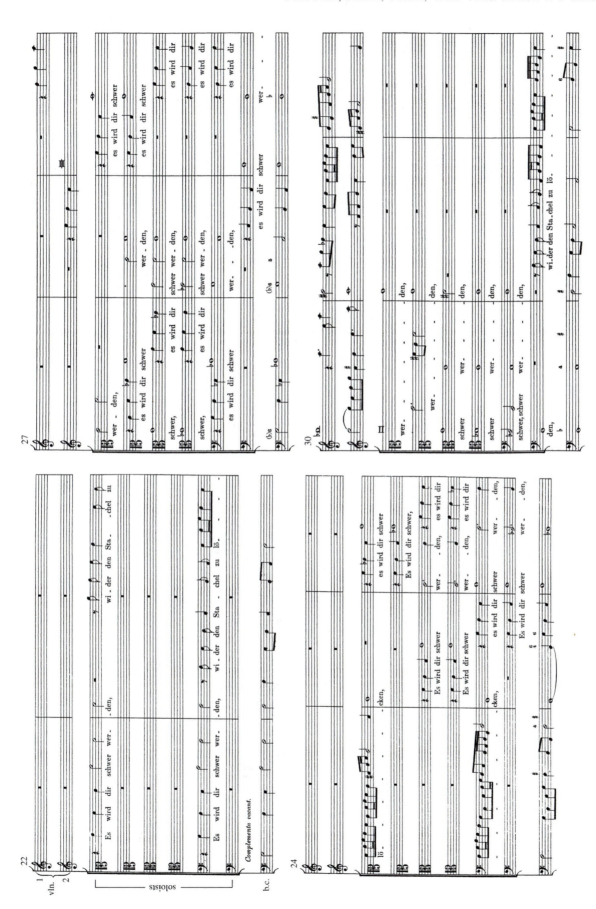

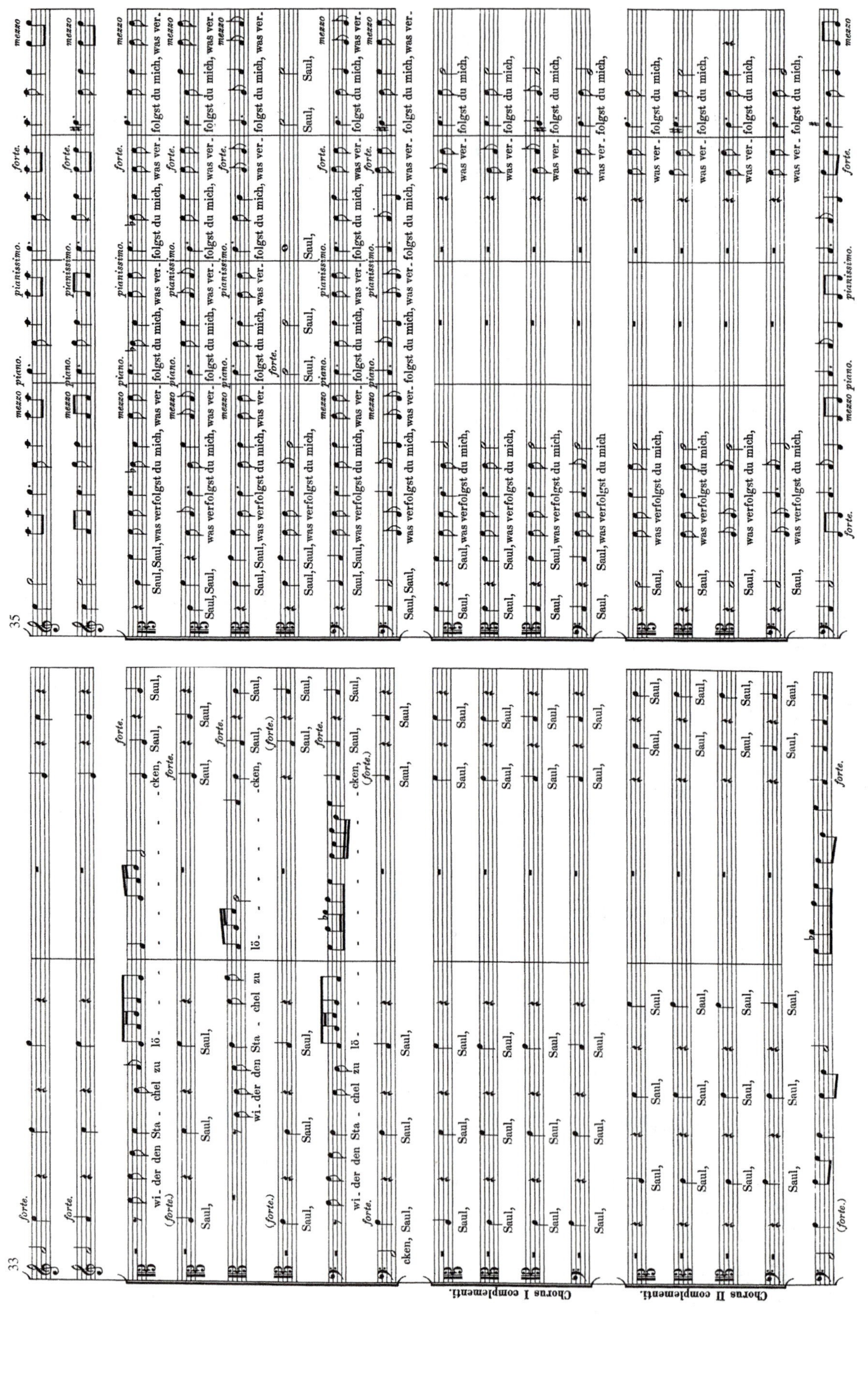
33
35
Chorus I complementi.
Chorus II complementi.
wi - der den Sta - chel zu lö - - - - - - - cken,
Saul, Saul, was verfolgst du mich, was ver - folgst du mich, was ver - folgst du mich, was ver -
forte.
mezzo piano.
pianissimo.
mezzo

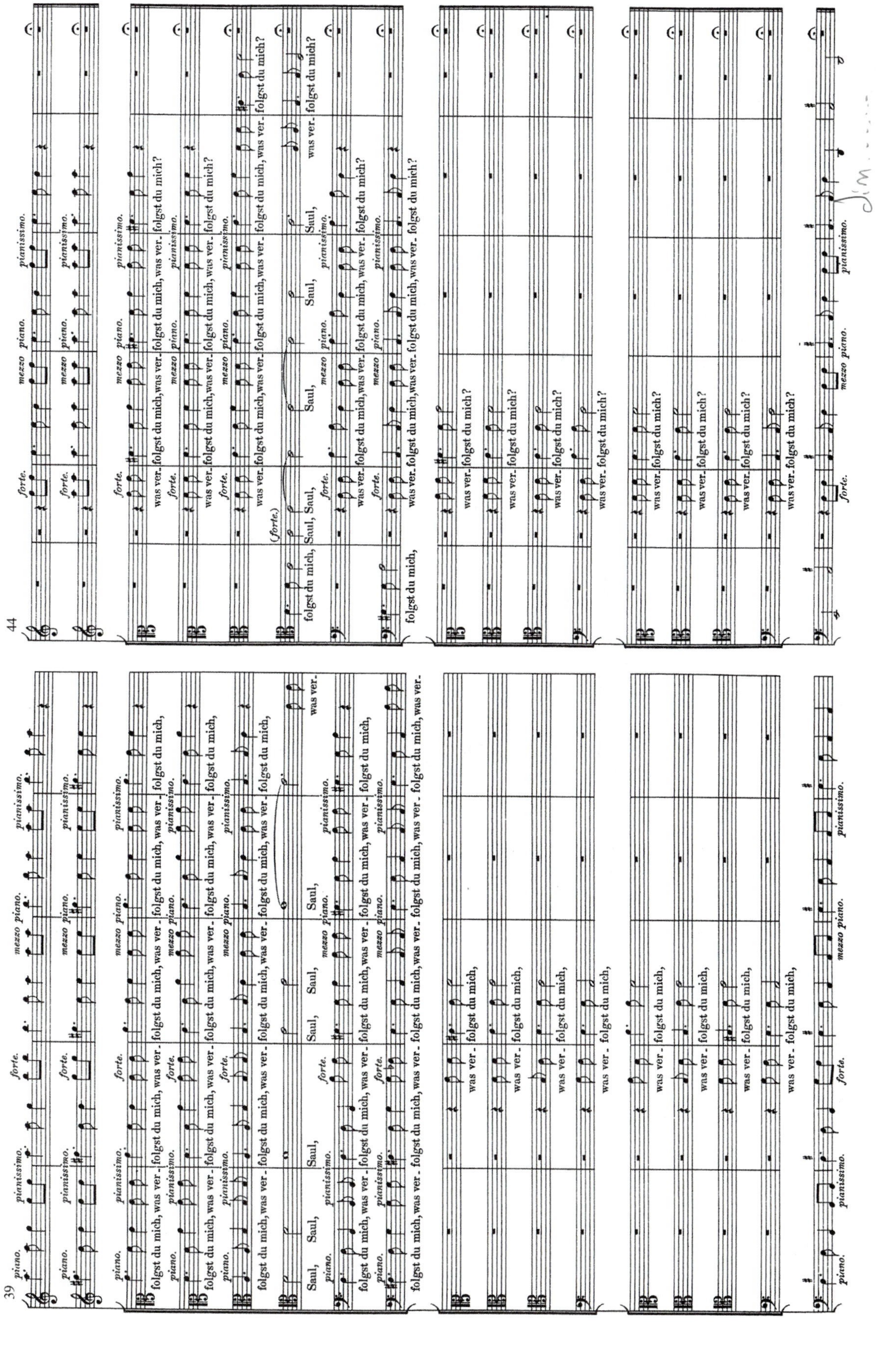
39
piano.
pianissimo.
forte.
mezzo piano.
folgst du mich, was ver - folgst du mich, was ver - folgst du mich, was ver - folgst du mich,
Saul, Saul, Saul, Saul, Saul, was ver-
was ver - folgst du mich,
44
(forte.)
folgst du mich, Saul, Saul, Saul, Saul, Saul,
was ver - folgst du mich, was ver - folgst du mich, was ver - folgst du mich?
was ver - folgst du mich?
dim.

TEXT AND TRANSLATION

1 Saul, Saul, was verfolgst du mich?   Saul, why do you persecute me?
2 Es wird dir schwer werden, wider   It will be difficult for you to kick against the
den Stachel zu lökken.   prods.

—Acts 26:14

EDITION

This score, like Selection 14, is reproduced from a nineteenth-century edition that, like other scholarly editions of the period, retained the original clefs and labels for the individual parts. The broad outlines of Schütz's polychoral score are nevertheless perfectly clear. The six principal vocal parts are joined by two violins (top two staves) and by two optional or *capella* choirs of four voices each, here designated *chori complementi* ("complementary choirs"). At the bottom of each system is the basso continuo.

PERFORMANCE ISSUES

As in Selection 13, the vocal and instrumental parts were probably not meant to be doubled, although Schütz again directs the use of "violone" together with organ on the basso continuo part. Modern performances often include trombones and other instruments that double or substitute for the voices of the capella choruses.

The two instrumental parts might be played not only by violins but by other "similar" instruments, by which Schütz might have had cornettos in mind. The time signatures again imply tempo relationships; three whole notes in the opening triple-time section were probably meant to be worth one whole note in the duple-time section beginning at measure 16. The dynamic markings are original; a series of closely spaced diminishing dynamics (as in mm. 11–12) seems to signify a decrescendo. From measure 36 to the end the tenor soloist remains *forte* while the other parts have repeated diminuendos from *forte* to *pianissimo*.

SOURCE

The score is reproduced from Heinrich Schütz: *Symphoniae sacrae: Dritter Theil, Zweite Abtheilung,* ed. Philipp Spitta, *Sämmtliche Werke* 11 (Leipzig, Germany: Breitkopf und Härtel, 1891), which derives from Schütz's *Symphonarum sacrarum tertia pars, opus 12* (Sacred symphonies, part 3, Dresden, 1650).

16. Giacomo Carissimi (1605–1674), *Jephte* (oratorio: selections)

TEXT AND TRANSLATION

Historicus

Cum autem victor Jephte
in domum suam reverteretur,
occurrens ei unigenita filia sua
cum tympanis et choris praecinebat:

Filia

Incipite in tympanis
Et psallite in cymbalis.
Hymnum cantemus Domino,
Et modulemur canticum.
Laudemus regem coelitum,
Laudemus belli principem,
Qui filiorum Israel
Victorem ducem reddidit.

Hymnum cantemus Domino,
Et modulemur canticum,
Qui dedit nobis gloriam
Et Israel victoriam.

. . .

Historicus

Cum videsset Jephte,
qui votum Domino voverat,
filiam suam venientem in occursum,
in dolore et lachrimis scidit
vestimenta sua et ait:

Jephte

Heu mihi! filia mea, heu
decepisti me, filia unigenita,
et tu pariter, heu filia mea
decepta es.

Filia

Cur ego te pater decepi,
et cur ego filia tua unigenita
  decepta sum?

Jephte

Aperui os meum ad Dominum,
ut quicumque primus de domo mea
occurrerit mihi offeram illum
Domino in holocaustum.
Heu mihi! filia mea, heu
decepisti me, filia unigenita,
et tu pariter, heu filia mea
decepta es.

—anonymous, after Judges 11:34–35

Narrator {bass}

When Jephtha had returned
victorious to his house,
running to him his only daughter
sang to him with timbrels and dances:

Daughter {soprano 1}

Take up the timbrels
And sound the cymbals.
We shall sing a hymn to the Lord
And make a song.
We shall praise the heavenly king,
We shall praise the prince of war
Who to the children of Israel
Has restored their victorious leader.

{Sopranos 2 and 3}

We shall sing a hymn
And make a song to the Lord,
Who has given us glory
And to Israel victory.

. . .

Narrator {alto}

When Jephtha,
who had sworn an oath to the Lord,
saw his daughter running to meet him,
with sadness and tears he tore
his clothes and said:

Jephtha {tenor}

Woe is me! my daughter, alas,
you have undone me, my only daughter,
and yourself as well; alas, my daughter,
you are undone.

Daughter

How, father, have I undone you,
and how am I, your only daughter,
  undone?

Jephtha

I have opened my mouth to the Lord,
that whoever first from my house
should run to me, I will offer him
to the Lord as a burnt offering.
Woe is me! my daughter, alas,
you have undone me, my only daughter,
and yourself as well; alas, my daughter,
you are undone.

PERFORMANCE ISSUES

The sopranos were probably adult male castrati, and the same voices that sang the solo parts of the Historicus, Jephtha, and his daughter also sang in the chorus; even in choral sections, the parts were probably not doubled. Most likely the continuo was played by organ alone, although in modern performances viola da gamba and theorbo are often included. Modern performances often use additional instruments to double the choral parts, which may be sung by multiple voices, but this is unlikely to have been Carissimi's intention.

SOURCE

This score is based on *Carissimi's Werke: Erste Abtheilung*, ed. Friedrich Chrysander, Denkmäler der Tonkunst, vol. 2 (Bergedorf, ca. 1869), corrected by consultation with the critical edition by Janet Beat (London: Novello, 1974), which follows a manuscript copy by the composer Marc-Antoine Charpentier as its principal source.

17. Michel-Richard de Lalande (1657–1726), *De profundis (grand motet,* Selections)

a. Chorus, *De profundis*

b. *Récit, Sustinuit anima mea*

TEXT AND TRANSLATION

De profundis clamavi ad te Domine: From the depths I cried to you, Lord:
Domine exaudi vocem meam.   Lord, hear my voice.

. . .   . . .

Sustinuit anima mea in verbo ejus: My soul has awaited your word;
speravit anima mea in Domino.   my soul has hoped in the Lord.

—Psalm 130:1–2a, 5

EDITION

These are the first and fifth movements from Lalande's nine-movement work. The score has been newly prepared from sources of the composer's revised version; the present fifth movement replaced a longer setting of the same text for the *petit chœur* in the first version (see below), and the opening movement also was somewhat shortened.

PERFORMANCE ISSUES

The part labels for the voices are those customary for the French *grand motet*. The *dessus* originally would probably have been boys or adult male falsettos, but later performances, including those of the Concert Spirituel, would have involved adult women. All of the lower vocal parts would have been sung by men. Multiple singers would have sung in the choral sections (mm. 44–94) of the opening movement, possibly reduced to smaller numbers (the *petit chœur*) in measures 53–54. The orchestra would have involved a similar division between large and small groups, the latter being employed perhaps during the initial baritone solo. The continuo part would have been similar to that of the opera, employing double-bass instruments (violones) only in performances of the later eighteenth century; reduced instrumentation would probably have been heard in passages sung by soloists or the *petit chœur*.

The signs for ornaments and for meter (time signatures) would have been interpreted as in other French music of the period, with *notes inégales* applied on eighth notes throughout both movements. Small notes (called *ports de voix* and *coulés*) would have been given fairly short values, but not as brief as modern grace notes. The distinction between the two different ornament signs used in the solo movement is not entirely clear, but whereas the trill symbol in measures 4–5 must stand for a brief ornament comprising a single repercussion, the cross or plus sign (+) probably refers to a longer trill, in most cases with a lengthened first (upper) note. The apparent chord for the voice in measure 41 of the first movement evidently provides an alternative for a soloist unable to reach the higher of the two notes.

SOURCES

The score has been prepared from the two main sources of the revised version, a vocal score published shortly after the composer's death (Paris: Boyvin, 1729) and a manuscript copy of the full score (Versailles, Bibliothèque Municipale, Ms. mus. 217, from the Cauvin collection, ca. 1741).[19] Although independent of one another, the sources contain many small errors; readings of ornaments and slurs have been taken from both of them.

---

[19]Both sources are published in facsimile: see Michel-Richard Delalande, *Grand motet: De profundis clamavi (Psaume 129)* (Courlay, France: Fuzeau, 1992).

18. George Frideric Handel (1685–1759), *Orlando* (opera: selections)

a. Act 1, scene 8 (recitative and aria "Oh care parolette")

b. Act 1, scene 9 (recitative and aria "Se fedel vuoi")

c. Act 1, scene 10 (recitative and aria "Fammi combattere")

dal mio va _ lor,

fammi com_bat_te_re mo_strie ti_fe _ i, no _ vi trofei se vuoi dal mio va_

_ lor.

Mu_ra glie ab_bat_te_re dis_fa_re in_can_ti, se vuoi ch'io van_ti dar ti pro _ ve d'a_mor,

(Fine.)

TEXT AND TRANSLATION

Act 1, scene 8

DORINDA SOLA	DORINDA ALONE

Dorinda

Povera me! Ben vedo che m'alletta
Con un parlar fallace;
Ma così ancor mi piace,
E ogni sua paroletta
Mi fa all'udito certa consonanza
Che accorda col desio pur la speranza.

[ARIA]

1 Oh care parolette, o dolci sguardi,
2 Sebben siete bugiardi
3 Tanto vi crederò.
4   Ma poi che far potrò,
5   Allor ch troppo tardi
6   Io vi concoscerò.
      Parte.

Act 1, scene 9

ZOROASTRO, ANGELICA, E POI
      ORLANDO

Zoroastro

Noti a me sono i tuoi fatali amori
Con Medoro; e non temi
La vendetta d'Orlando?

Angelica

                É ver, che devo
Molto all'eroe, ma—

Zoroastro

                Già sen vien! Celato
Mi terrò per vegliar d'ognuno al fato.

      Si ritira a parte.

Orlando *in disparte*

Quando mai troverò l'orme fugaci
D'Angelica la bella?

Angelica

Oh Dei, se vien Medoro,
Che quì attendea per partir seco! Eh
  forse,
Se Orlando qua conduce il novo amore
Per quella ch'ei salvò da man nemica,

Non sarà così grande il mio timore.

Dorinda

Poor me! I know I am allured
By his deceptive speech;
But thusly he still pleases me,
And each of his little words
Makes, when I hear it, a certain harmony
That tunes my hopes to my desires.

Oh, dear words, sweet looks,
Though you are liars,
I shall still believe you!
      But then what shall I do,
      When, too late,
      I see through you?
She leaves.

ZOROASTER AND ANGELICA, THEN
      ORLANDO

Zoraster

I am aware of your fatal love
For Medoro; don't you fear
Orlando's vengeance?

Angelica

                It's true that I owe
Much to the hero, yet—

Zoroastro

                But he's coming! Concealed,
I shall keep watching over each one's
  destiny.
He withdraws.

Orlando *(aside)*

Whenever shall I find the fleeting traces
Of fair Angelica?

Angelica

Oh Gods, if Medoro should come,
He whom I was awaiting here to leave with
  him! If only
A new love were to conduct Orlando
Toward her whom he saved from an enemy
  hand,
My fear would be less great.

Vo' fingermi gelosa	I shall feign jealousy,
Per meglio discoprire il suo pensiero.	The better to discover his thoughts.
Si presenta ad Orlando.	*She stands before Orlando.*
Orlando, ed è pur vero	Orlando, is it true
Ch'io qui ti veda!	That I see you here?

Orlando

Oh Cieli! Oh cara, e come	Oh heavens! my dear, how
Potevo mai sperar sì lieta sorte!	Could I ever hope for such good fortune?
Angelica, mio bene.	Angelica, my love.

Angelica

Erri nel nome,	You err in the name;
Isabella vuoi dir, che là t'attende.	You mean Isabella, who awaits you here.

Orlando

Son della principessa	I am that princess's
Difensor, non amante.	Defender, not her lover.

Angelica

Ma per tale ti pubblicò Dorinda	But that is what Dorinda called you,
Allora, e quando——	Then, and when——

Orlando

Un'Angelica sol può amare Orlando.	Orlando can love only Angelica.

Angelica

vedendo Medoro da lontano	*seeing Medoro in the distance*
(Ma, oh dei! vedo Medor!	(But, oh gods, I see Medoro!
Convien che Orlando allontani di qua.)	It is necessary that Orlando leave from here.)
Esce il mago facendo segno colla verga, sorge di sotterra una gran fontana, che copre Medoro, la scena cangiandosi in un delizioso giardino.	*The magician comes forth waving his wand, and a great fountain rises from beneath the earth, concealing Medoro as the scene changes to a delightful garden.*

Orlando

Chiedimi o bella	Ask, my dear,
Nuove prove d'amore.	For new proofs of my love

Angelica

(O soccorso opportun!) Sentimi Orlando	(What good luck!) Hear me, Orlando,
Se pur vuoi, ch'io ti creda	If you would like me to think you are
A me fedel; pronto da te allontana	Faithful to me, immediately separate yourself from
La dama, che a color di mano hai tolto,	That lady whom you once took from them,
O non vedrai d'Angelica più il volto.	Or you shall never again see Angelica.

[ARIA]

1 Se fedel vuoi, ch'io ti creda	If you want me to trust in your faith,
2 Fa che veda	Do something to show
3 La tua fedeltà.	Your faithfulness.
4 Finchè regni nel mio petto	As long as my thoughts are ruled by Suspicion,
5 Il sospetto,	
6 Mai l'amor vi regnerà.	Love shall never rule.
Parte.	*She leaves.*

Act 1, scene 10

ORLANDO SOLO	ORLANDO ALONE

Orlando

Orlando

T'ubbidirò, crudele,	I will obey you, cruel one,
E vedrai in questo istante,	And you shall see in this instant
Che della principessa	That of the princess
Fui solo difensor, ma non amante.	I was the defender, not the lover.

[ARIA]

1 Fammi combattere	Make me combat
2 Mostri e tifei,	Monsters and demons,
3 Novi trofei	If new trophies
4 Se vuoi dal mio valor.	You want of my valor.
5 Muraglie abbattere	Obstacles must be demolished,
6 Disfare incanti,	I must defeat enchantments,
7 Se vuoi ch'io vanti	If you want me to boast
8 Darti prove d'amor.	That I have given you proofs of my love.
Parte.	*He leaves.*

—after Carlo Sigismondo Capeci

EDITION

Our score is taken from a nineteenth-century edition that closely reflects Handel's manuscript. Thus, as in many eighteenth-century composers' scores, the rather sketchy information about instrumentation given in the heading of each movement must be supplemented from clues within the body of the music.

In Dorinda's aria, the label *tutti unisoni* (literally, "all in unison") actually means violins 1 and 2, doubled by oboes. The oboes are silent in the *piano* passages, reentering in the *forte* passages marked *Tutti*. Similarly, the *bassi* (bass instruments) include, besides cellos, a double bass and perhaps one or two bassoons that drop out when the part is notated in tenor clef or where *pianissimo* is indicated. Possibly one of the two harpsichords often employed in eighteenth-century opera dropped out at these points as well.

Handel left no indications of scoring for Angelica's aria, but the editor's parenthesized suggestions are surely correct. The continuo part in the recitatives was probably intended for a single harpsichord, possibly with a cello doubling the bass line.

PERFORMANCE ISSUES

Some of the basic conventions of late Baroque Italian vocal performance, such as those involving recitative and the decoration of da capo arias, are explained in the text volume (see the discussion of Ex. 5.6). In the recitatives, the notes of the bass line would not have been held out as written but rather released after a beat or two. The harpsichordist might have emphasized certain words by decorating the accompanying chords with arpeggios.

Our edition alters the notation of final cadences in the recitatives, suggesting that the penultimate (dominant) bass note should be delayed until after the voice has sung its last two notes (see e.g., the final measure in each of the three recitative sections). This does not appear to have been normal practice in Italian opera during Handel's lifetime, despite the harmonic clash that results when, following convention, the singer alters the penultimate note (at the end of her recitative, Dorinda would have sung d″–a′ against the harpsichord's A-major harmony).

Orlando's part was written for the alto castrato Senesino. Modern performances generally choose between an adult male falsetto singer and a female mezzo-soprano. Transposing the part an octave downward, for a baritone, would cause it to pass close to and even beneath the bass line in several passages. This would muddy the texture and dull the brilliance of the coloratura.

The tempo marking *Largo* (literally, "broad") for Angelica's aria does not necessarily indicate a particularly slow tempo. It may allude rather to a spacious, sustained style for both the singer and the string orchestra. The word *adagio* in measure 15 is probably a suggestion not only for a ritard but also for some improvised embellishment by the singer.

SOURCE

The edition is that of Georg Friedrich Händel, *Werke*, vol. 82, *Orlando*, ed. Friedrich Chrysander (Leipzig: Deutsche Händelgesellschaft, 1881), which was based primarily on the autograph score (London, British Library, R.M. 20.b.8).

19. Jean-Philippe Rameau (1683–1764), *Les indes galantes* (*opéra-ballet*: selections)

TEXT AND TRANSLATION

Nouvelle entrée, scene 4 {conclusion}

ON ENTEND UN PRÉLUDE QUI ANNONCE
LA FÊTE

A PRELUDE IS HEARD, ANNOUNCING
THE FESTIVITIES.

Damon

Déjà, dans les bois d'alentour,
J'entends de nos guerriers les bruyantes
trompettes.
Leurs sons n'effrayent plus ces aimables
retraites;
Des charmes de la paix ils marquent le
retour.
(*à Alvar*)
À vos tristes regrets dérobez ce beau jour!

Que le plaisir avec nous vous arrête!

Already, in the surrounding woods,
I hear the loud trumpets of our warriors.

Their sounds no longer terrify these
pleasant retreats;
They mark the return of the charms of
peace.
(*to Alvar*)
Rescue this beautiful day from your sad
regrets!
Let pleasure hold you here with us!

Alvar

(s'éloignant)

Hélas! Je vais cacher un malheureux
    amour.

(leaving)

Alas, I go to conceal an unfortunate love.

Damon

(le suivant)

Venez plutôt l'amuser à la fête!

(following him)

Come instead to amuse it at the festivities!

SCENE 5: *ADARIO, ZIMA*

Adario

Je ne vous peindrai point les transports
    de mon cœur,
Belle Zima, jugez-en par le vôtre!
En comblant mon bonheur
Vous montrez qu'une égale ardeur
Nous enflamme l'un et l'autre.

I shall not describe to you the raptures of
    my heart,
Beautiful Zima; judge them by your own!
Redoubling my good fortune,
You show that equal ardor
Enflames us both.

Zima

De l'amour le plus tendre éprouvez la
    douceur!
Je vous dois la préférence.
De vous à vos rivaux je vois la
    différence:
L'un s'abandonne à la fureur,
Et l'autre perd mon cœur avec
    indifférence.
Nous ignorons ce calme et cette
    violence.

Feel the sweetness of the most tender
    love!
To you I owe my preference.
Between you and your rivals I see the
    difference:
The one abandons himself to passion,
And the other loses my heart with
    indifference.
We do not know this calmness nor this
    violence.

{ARIA}

1 Sur nos bords l'amour vole et prévient
    nos désirs.
2 Dans notre paisible retraite
3 On n'entend murmurer que l'onde et
    les zéphyrs;
4 Jamais l'écho n'y répête
5 De nos regrets ni de soupirs.

Above our shores, love flies and anticipates
    our desires.
In our peaceable retreat
One hears murmuring only the wave and
    the breezes;
Never does an echo there repeat
Either our regrets or our sighs.

Adario

Viens, Hymen, hâte-toi, suis l'amour qui
    t'appelle.

Come, Hymen,[20] make haste, follow Love,
    who calls you.

Zima, Adario

{Duet}

1 Hymen, viens nous unir d'une chaîne
    éternelle!
2 Viens encore de la paix embellir les
    beaux jours!
3 Viens! je te promets d'être fidèle.

Hymen, come join us with an eternal
    bond!
Come again to embellish with peace these
    fair days!
Come; I promise you I will be faithful.

---

[20]In ancient Greek religion, Hymen was the god of marriage.

| 4 Tu sais nous enchaîner et nous plaire toujours. | You know how to bind us and to delight us forever. |
| 5 Viens! je te promets d'être fidèle. | Come; I promise you I will be faithful. |

—Louis Fuzelier

EDITION

This score is from an early twentieth-century edition that includes an editorial reduction of the instrumental parts, intended for playing on the piano when an orchestra is not available. This piano reduction appears in small print on the bottom two staves of each system, except in the recitatives, where these staves contain an editorial realization of the figured bass. Slurs and ornaments are mostly original, as are tempo and dynamic indications. A number of indications for tempo and instrumentation appear in parentheses; they seem to derive from secondary manuscript sources (see below).

The names of the instruments and the singing characters are given in abbreviated form: *Fl.* = *flûte*, that is recorder; H^b = *hautbois* (oboe); B^{ons} = bassoons; *Tromp.* = trumpet; *Timb.* = timpani; V^{ons} = violins; *Alt.* = viola; *D.* = Damon; *A.* = first Alvar, then Adario; *Z.* = Zima.

PERFORMANCE ISSUES

The brief *prélude* (mm. 1–4) is for the full orchestra of the French royal opera, which at this date included numerous players on the three upper string parts; the woodwind parts might have been doubled as well. The basso continuo would have been played by several cellos and one or two harpsichords, reinforced by double bass (the bassoon doubling is written out in our score). In Zima's air, a smaller group of violins probably played, and the continuo was probably more lightly scored here, as it certainly was in the recitatives and the closing duet.

Most of the ornamentation—trills and appoggiaturas of various types—has been written out, and there is little room for additional improvised decoration. The conventions that governed tempo in the older works of Lully and Charpentier must still have applied in the recitative sections, which show the changing time signatures typical of French Baroque vocal music. Thus the half note of the sections in "2" probably has the same value as a quarter note in the sections in "3" and in "C." But tempo in the *prélude* and in the duet is signified by verbal indications (in French), and that of Zima's aria is implied by its gavotte rhythm.

SOURCE

The edition, by the composer Paul Dukas (1865–1935), was published as volume 7 of Jean-Philippe Rameau, *Œuvres complètes* (Paris: Durand, 1902). Some of the individual volumes in this series are notoriously unreliable, adding inauthentic wind parts and other features, but the present score is derived closely from the first edition of the fourth *entrée*.[21]

---

[21]*Les indes galantes: Balet {sic} reduit a {sic} quatre grands concerts* (Paris: Boivin et al., 1736). As the title indicates, this print contained only selections from the work as a whole, but it included the complete fourth *entrée*.

20. Johann Sebastian Bach (1685–1750), *Herr Jesu Christ, wahr' Mensch und Gott*, BWV 127 (sacred cantata)

2. Recitativo

Wenn Al - les sich zur letz - ten Zeit ent - setz - et, Und wenn ein

kal - ter To - des - schweiss Die schon er - starr - ten Glie - der netz - et, Wenn

mei - ne Zun - ge nichts, als nur durch Seuf - zer spricht, Und

die - ses Her - ze bricht: Ge - nug, dass da der Glau - be weiss, Dass

Je - sus bei mir steht, Der mit Ge - duld zu sei - nem Lei - den geht Und die - sen schwe - ren

Weg auch mich ge - lei - tet, Und mir die Ru - - - he zu - be - rei - tet.

3. Aria

Da capo

5. Choral

TEXT AND TRANSLATION

I.   *{Chorus}*

1 Herr Jesu Christ, wahr'r Mensch und   Lord Jesus Christ, true man and God,
   Gott

2 Der du litt'st Marter, Angst und Spott,   You who suffered martyrdom, pain, and scorn,

3 Für mich am Kreuz auch endlich   [And who] for me on the cross finally died,
   starbst,

4 Und mir dein's Vaters Huld erwarbst,   And for me your father's grace earned,

5 Ich bitt' durch's bitt're Leiden dein: I pray, by your bitter suffering:

6 Du woll'st mir Sünder gnädig sein.   To me, a sinner, be merciful.

II. [Recitativo]   *[Recitative]*

1 Wenn Alles sich zur letzten Zeit   When everything, in the final time,
   entsetzet,   is destroyed,

2 Und wenn ein kalter Todesschweiss   And when a cold deathly sweat

3 Die schon erstarrten Glieder netzet,   The already stiff limbs enwraps,

4 Wenn meine Zunge nichts, als nur   When my tongue nothing but sighs speaks,
   durch Seufzer spricht,

5 Und dieses Herze bricht: And this heart breaks:

6 Genug, dass da der Glaube weiss,   [It is] enough that [my] belief knows

7 Dass Jesus bei mir steht,   That Jesus by me stands,

8 Der mit Geduld zu seinem Leiden   [He] who with patience to his suffering
   geht   goes

9 Und diesen schweren Weg auch mich   And [along] this hard path leads even me,
   geleitet,

10 Und mir die *Ruhe zubereitet.*   And for me *rest prepares.*

III. Aria   *Aria*

1 Die Seele ruht in Jesu Händen   The soul rests in Jesus' hands
2 Wenn Erde diesen Leib bedeckt.   Though earth this body covers.
3   Ach, ruft mich bald, ihr   Ah, call me soon, you
          Sterbeglocken,   funeral bells,
4   Ich bin zum Sterben unerschrocken   I am of death unafraid
5   Weil mich mein Jesus wiederweckt.   So long as my Jesus reawakens me.

IV. [Recitativo ed Aria]   *[Recitative and Aria]*

1 Wenn einstens die Posaunen schallen,   When one day the trumpet sounds
2 Und wenn der Bau der Welt   And when the span of the world,

3 Nebst denen Himmels-Vesten	With its high solemnities
4 Zerschmettert wird zerfallen,	Shattered, falls to pieces,
5 So denke, mein Gott, im Besten:	Then think, my God, the best [of me]:
6 Wenn sich dein Knecht einst vor's Gerichte stellt,	When your servant before the court of judgment stands,
7 Da die Gedanken sich verklagen,	When [his own] thoughts accuse him,
8 So wollest du allein,	Then let you alone,
9 O Jesu, mein Fürsprecher sein,	O Jesus, be my advocate,
10 Und meiner Seele tröstlich sagen:	And to my soul comfortingly say:
11 Fürwahr, euch sage ich:	Behold, to you I say:
12 Wenn Himmel und Erde im Feuer vergehen	Though heaven and earth in fire [will] disappear
13 So soll doch ein Gläubiger ewig stehen.	[Even] then will a believer forever stand.
14 Er wird nicht kommen in's Gericht	He will not be condemned
15 Und den Tod ewig schmecken nicht,	And eternal death he will not taste;
16 Nur halte dich, mein Kind, an mich:	Only, my child, hold fast to me.
17 Ich breche mit starker und helfender Hand	I break, with a strong and merciful hand,
18 Des Todes gewaltig geschlossenes Band.	Of death the powerful encompassing bond.
Fürwahr, euch sage ich . . .	

V. Choral

Chorale

1 Ach Herr, vergieb all' unsre Schuld,	Oh Lord, forgive all our sin,
2 Hilf, dass wir warten mit Geduld,	Help us to wait with patience
3 Bis unser Stündlein kömmt herbei,	Until our time comes by,
4 Auch unser Glaub' stets wacker sei,	Let our belief always be stronger,
5 Dein'm Wort zu trauen festiglich,	In your word trusting firmly
6 Bis wir einschlafen seliglich.	Until we fall asleep blessedly.

EDITION

This score derives from Bach's original manuscript score and parts. Clefs have been modernized, but otherwise the notation is very close to Bach's.

At Leipzig, the organ was tuned a step higher than the other instruments, and its lowest sounding note was D (written C). Therefore, where the continuo part descends to low C, the bass of the organ part, which normally doubles the cello, is instead an octave higher; the few instances where this occurs (e.g., first movement, m. 9) are not shown in this score.[22] The ornament sign originally occurring in the fourth movement at measure 10 (voice, fourth beat) has been written out in small notes.

PERFORMANCE ISSUES

The historical performance of Bach's cantatas has been investigated more thoroughly than that of perhaps any other early repertory, leading to discoveries that have provoked controversy in modern times, even though in most cases Bach's practices did not differ from those of his contemporaries. In particular, it has become clear in recent years that most of these works were composed for vocal forces consisting of a single singer on each part. The instruments, too, were rarely doubled, with the exception of the violin and continuo parts.

For this work, not only do we have Bach's original composing score; the manuscript parts copied from it for the first performance in 1725 also survive. Nevertheless, the apparent haste with which the latter were copied leaves unclear many of Bach's detailed intentions regarding performance. For instance, many slurs, ornament signs, and other performance markings, including most of the figures for the organ part, are missing. In addition, the loss of the trumpet part leaves open the possibility that this instrument doubled the soprano (the chorale melody) in the outer movements. To do so, however, the player of the valveless trumpet of Bach's day would have had to replace the normal mouthpiece with a slide mechanism, in order to sound notes that lie outside the harmonic series.

In addition, the music raises many issues that arise in other Baroque works. For example, the dotted eighth notes of the first movement might be "overdotted." The written-out melodic embellishment of the soprano aria sounds best when performed with rhythmic freedom, suggesting improvisation, although this freedom might be applied only to the smaller values. There is little room for real improvisation, but ornaments such as trills might be added at conventionally appropriate places (e.g., movement 3, m. 26, oboe, b♮ on beat 4). The fermata at measure 29 in the third movement is merely the equivalent of the word *fine* ("end," that is, after repeating the A section), and the fermatas in the concluding chorale movement may have been merely a way of indicating the ends of phrases. But it is possible that short pauses were indeed taken at these fermatas, and in some places there was a tradition of organists' inserting cadenzas at

---

[22]Bach's organist played from a transposing part; thus the organ part for the cantata would have shown the opening movement in E♭ instead of F. Compare Figure 9.3 in the text volume, which includes a part notated in G minor for an aria in A minor.

these points during the congregational singing of chorales. The congregation probably would not, however, have joined in the singing of a chorale movement within a cantata at Leipzig.

SOURCE

This edition is based on the score that Bach evidently completed before the first performance of this work on 11 February 1725 and on the original performing parts copied from it.[23]

---

[23]Score, plus duplicate violin and continuo parts: Berlin, Staatsbibliothek, Mus. mss. Bach P 872 and St 393; microfiche reproduction: *Musikhandschriften der Staatsbibliothek zu Berlin, Preussischer Kulturbesitz. Teil 1, Bach-Sammlung* (Munich: Saur Verlag, 2000). Additional parts: Leipzig, Bach-Archiv, Thomaner 127.

21. George Frideric Handel (1685–1759), *Jephtha* (English oratorio: selections)

a. From Part 2, scene 3

con _ quest gain, ere I the ___ name of ___ fa _ ther stain, and deepest woe from con _ quest gain.
Sieg mir trug, eh' mir mein Va _ ter _ na _ me Fluch, und bit_tres Weh der Sieg mir trug.

b. **From Part 2, scene 4**

TEXT

a. From Part 2, scene 3

Jephtha

Horror! confusion! harsh this music grates	
Upon my tasteless* ears. —Be gone, my child,	*unable to sense anything pleasurable
Thou hast undone the father. Fly, be gone,	
And leave me to the rack* of wild despair.	*torment

[ARIA]

1 Open thy marble jaws, O tomb,
2 And hide me, earth, in thy dark womb!
3   Ere I the name of father stain,
4   And deepest woe from conquest gain.

b. From Part 2, scene 4

Chorus

 1 How dark, O Lord, are thy decrees!
 2 All hid from mortal sight!
 3 All our joys to sorrow turning,
 4 And our triumphs into mourning,
 5 As the night succeeds the day.
 6 No certain bliss,
 7 No solid peace,
 8 We mortals know
 9 On earth below.
10 Yet on this maxim still obey:
11 Whatever is, is right.

—Thomas Morell (with additions)

EDITION

As with Handel's *Orlando* (Selection 18), our score is from the nineteenth-century edition of the composer's complete works. It is based on Handel's autograph manuscript, but the bottom two staves of each system contain the editor's piano arrangement of the orchestral parts; in the recitative and aria these staves incorporate an editorial continuo realization. The dynamic indications in this part are also editorial.

In Jephtha's aria, *violini unisoni* means that the two violin parts play together at the beginning (but they divide in the B section). The staff designated "Bassi" by the editor is the continuo part, but in the chorus the word *Basso* refers to the bass voices of the choir. In the choral movement, the lower strings play along with the keyboard continuo on the part designated *Organo* (organ).

PERFORMANCE ISSUES

Handel would have employed a number of boy sopranos for the top part, plus several adult men on each of the three lower parts (altos singing the higher notes falsetto).[24] Continuo for the recitative was perhaps confined to harpsichord, possibly joined by a single cello. The orchestra would have employed several players on each of the string

---

[24]Although the top choral staff is labeled *Canto I. II.*, there is only one soprano part.

parts; in the aria, the violas probably doubled the continuo an octave higher. An organ presumably entered with the choir in the chorus.

The style and dramatic situation of Jephtha's aria clearly make improvisatory embellishment inappropriate. But at least a few cadential trills would surely have been heard (e.g., on f♯ in m. 53). Handel's tempo mark for the aria is unusually precise for a Baroque work ("With spirit, but not quick"). In the chorus, on the other hand, *largo*, which literally means "broad," might signify a spacious sort of performance but not necessarily a very slow one. *Larghetto* is probably somewhat faster; *a tempo ordinario* ("at regular speed") refers to a moderate pace that was thought appropriate to solemn or weighty movements. In the final section, the repeated notes in the strings bear slurs (in mm. 114–15). These slurs, which should probably be extended to the entire section, signify a Baroque technique known as bow vibrato (or slurred tremolo), in which the repetitions are produced by rhythmically pressing the stick (wood) of the bow with the first finger of the right hand, without any cessation of sound.

SOURCE

The edition is reproduced from Georg Friedrich Händel, *Jephtha: Oratorium*, ed. Friedrich Chrysander, *Werke*, vol. 44 (Leipzig: Deutsche Händelgesellschaft, 1886), which is based primarily on the composer's autograph score.[25]

---

[25] London, British Library, R.M. 20.e.9 (see Fig. 9.5 in the text volume); the editor Chrysander had published a now-rare facsimile edition in 1885 (Hamburg: Deutsche Händelgesellschaft).

22. Ennemond Gaultier (1575–1651), Pieces for Lute

a. Courante "L'immortelle"

b. Allemande (*Tombeau de Mesangeau*)

c. Gigue "La Poste"

EDITION

Seventeenth-century lute music was normally written in tablature, a type of notation that is legible to few other than lute players (see Fig. 10.3 in the text volume). This edition is based on one of the few seventeenth-century examples of score notation for the lute, from a French publication by an editor known only as Perrine. Some features of Perrine's rhythmic notation have been altered for easier reading, but no notes or actual pitches have been changed. Not included in the present score are the indications for right-hand lute fingering given both by Perrine and in manuscript copies notated in lute tablature. A few bracketed notes and other entries have been added by analogy to readings in tablature sources.

The gigue is better known as an allemande; Perrine gives both versions, although they differ only slightly, as is evident from the opening of the version as an allemande, shown below:

The gigue version contains a greater number of dotted rhythms, implying somewhat livelier performance. Evidently there was a tradition of playing certain pieces as both allemandes and gigues, and it is possible that the gigue as edited by Perrine was his own creation.

PERFORMANCE ISSUES

The score includes three ornament signs, only one of which Perrine explains: the diagonal line (/) stands for a *séparé*, a measured breaking of the chord. Two other signs can be understood by comparison with other French sources: the letter x apparently indicates a trill (*tremblement*), and a curved line or small arc beneath a note represents a *port de voix* or a *pincé* (the two ornaments were often combined; see Selection 29). Another ornament distinctive to the idiom of the lute is written out in notes at the beginning of the gigue: the simultaneous striking of two notes a half step apart, producing a biting dissonance before the lower note moves up to form a unison. Because the two notes are slurred, that is, played without replucking the string for the second note, the latter is always quieter than the first (dissonant) one. The examples below illustrate possible realizations of the ornament signs in the *tombeau*, measures 6–7, and the gigue, measures 5–6.

It is sometimes thought that the quadruple meter of the gigue would have been converted in performance to compound meter ($\frac{12}{8}$). But exactly how this would have been done is unclear, and no Baroque source describes the practice. The issue recurs in gigues by Froberger (see Selection 24).

SOURCE

The present score has been newly prepared after comparison with a modern facsimile of Perrine, *Pièces de luth en musique* (Paris, 1680).[26]

---

[26]Geneva, Switzerland: Minkoff Reprint, 1982. Perrine's collection appears in a modern edition by Paola Erdas (Bologna, Italy: Ut Orpheus Edizioni, 1995). For transcriptions of Gaultier's works as they appear in manuscript tablatures, see *Œuvres du vieux Gautier*, edited by André Souris, with historical introduction and lists of concordances by Monique Rollin, second edition (Paris: Éditions du Centre National de la Recherche Scientifique, 1980).

23. Girolamo Frescobaldi (1583–1643), Toccata 7 (from *Libro* II)

EDITION

This work was originally published in the standard Italian keyboard notation of the sixteenth and seventeenth centuries: two staves, as in modern notation, but with six and eight lines, respectively, on the upper and lower staves. This edition retains the original, irregular barlines but adds dotted barlines where appropriate in modern common time.

PERFORMANCE ISSUES

The performing medium is specified in the title of the collection in which the toccata first appeared: harpsichord or organ. Frescobaldi's first book (*Libro* I) of toccatas and partitas included a preface in which the composer described a number of points about its performance. He mentions in particular the need to vary the tempo in accordance with the affect or expressive character of each passage, and the use of small pauses or ritards at cadences and at the ends of written-out embellishments. Other contemporary treatises describe such matters as fingering and the performance of trills (*groppi*) and other ornaments, many of which were written out by the composer in this piece.

SOURCE

This score has been newly prepared for this edition. The work was first published in Frescobaldi's *Il secondo libro di toccate . . . d'intavolatura di cembalo et organo* (Rome, 1627); a second edition appeared in 1637.[27]

---

[27]For a facsimile of the 1637 edition, see Girolamo Frescobaldi, *Il secondo libro di toccate: Roma 1637*, ed. Laura Alvini (Florence, Italy: Studio per Edizioni Scelte, 1978).

24. Johann Jacob Froberger (1616–1667), Suite 20 in D

Meditation sur ma mort future

NB Memento Mori Froberger?

EDITION

This edition, newly prepared for the present volume, closely follows three seventeenth-century manuscripts: a recently discovered autograph and a recently discovered copy in Berlin as well as a copy of the first movement by the composer's pupil Matthias Weckmann. All three manuscripts add at the end of the first movement the comment "Memento mori Froberger?" (Remember, Froberger, that you must die?); the copy in Berlin adds an indication that Froberger composed the piece in Paris on 1 May 1660. An inacurate posthumous edition (first issued ca. 1698) moves the gigue to the end of the suite and includes other unlikely readings.

PERFORMANCE ISSUES

Like much Baroque keyboard music preserved primarily in manuscript, Froberger's suite contains only a few ornament signs. Precisely what ornaments would have been used in

1660 is uncertain, but they would have broadly resembled those indicated in later French-style keyboard music (see Selection 29). The precise nature of the instruments for which Froberger conceived the piece is also uncertain, but his first choice was probably a type of harpsichord fairly close to the French-style harpsichords of the eighteenth century that have been widely reproduced in our own time—as opposed to the more strident but less resonant Italian instruments of the seventeenth and eighteenth centuries.

Tempo was largely dictated by the traditional characteristics of the four dances drawn on in this suite. The opening "Meditation" is an example of an allemande, but the allemande was no longer a true dance during Froberger's lifetime. The title alone would suggest that this movement is to be played freely, like an improvised prelude. The manuscripts consulted for this edition add that the piece is to be "played slowly and with *discrétion*"—the last word refering to rhythmic freedom. A letter written by Froberger's last patron and pupil, Duchess Sibylla of Württemberg-Montbéliard, referring to this very piece, asserts that only those who have heard the composer play this music can themselves perform it with "proper discretion." The Berlin manuscript is the source for a similar marking at the point where the gigue returns to the style of the allemande (m. 18).

It is sometimes thought that in gigues such as the present one, notated in common time, the pervasive dotted rhythms were actually performed as triplets (i.e., triplet quarter followed by triplet eighth). There is no contemporary evidence for altering the notated meter of such a piece, although a few of Froberger's gigues exist in two versions, one in common time, one in compound time (that is, with dotted rhythms replaced by triplets). This gigue is known only in the present version.

The last two movements both bear the time signature "C3." In principle this was actually a sign for a proportional tempo relationship, but by Froberger's day it was evidently equivalent to the modern time signature $\frac{6}{4}$, or $\frac{3}{2}$ in the hemiolic measures of the courante (e.g., mm. 2–3, 6).

SOURCES

The autograph consulted for the present edition was sold at auction in 2006 and its whereabouts are not publicly known. The Berlin manuscript, whose readings are close to those of the autograph, has been published in both facsimile and an accurate transcription.[28]

---

[28]See *Johann Jacob Froberger: Toccaten, Suiten, Lamenti. Die Handschrift SA 4450 der Sing-Akademie zu Berlin: Faksimile und Übertragung*, 2d edition, ed. Peter Wollny and the Sing-Akademie zu Berlin (Berlin: Bärenreiter, 2006). I am grateful to harpsichordist Bob van Asperen for sharing with me his notes on readings in the autograph of Suite 20.

25. Elizabeth-Claude Jacquet de La Guerre (1665–1729),
Prélude from Suite 3 in A minor

EDITION

This score is a close transcription of the original printed edition. A number of slurs, including the first two, have been redrawn at points where in the original engraving there appear to be extra slurs or slurs are placed wrongly. The two left-hand notes at the beginning of the piece are shown as they appear in the source, but it is possible that both were meant to be played before the right hand begins. Near the end of the eighth system, the original notated values of e″ and d″ (quarter–whole), have been reversed, since e″, not d″, is the chord tone.

PERFORMANCE ISSUES

This is a relatively short and simple example of an unmeasured prelude, which requires the player not only to find a convincing rhythmic interpretation of the notation but also to interpret the slurs. The actual meaning of the slurs is to extend the value of the notes to which they are attached; thus the first two notes in the lower staff continue to sound until the next bass note is struck. Tones written as whole notes are chord tones that might be held for any duration; apparent quarter notes are usually passing notes inserted within broken chords, whereas eighths and sixteenths are written-out ornaments and embellishments. Slurs not only indicate the holding out of notes but may also group together notes belonging to a single harmony. A few ornaments are indicated by symbols: the cross or plus sign (+) represents an appoggiatura, or *port de voix*, whereas the mordent, or *pincé*, is indicated by the customary squiggle cut by a slash (as on the second note of the lower staff).

SOURCE

This score has been newly prepared from the first edition (long believed to have been lost): *Pieces de clavecin de Mad* ᵉˡˡᵉ *de La Guerre . . . Premier Livre* (Paris, 1687), which is available in facsimile (Elisabeth Jacquet de La Guerre, *Les pièces de clavessin: Premier livre*, with introduction by Carol Bates, Geneva, Switzerland: Minkoff, 1996).

26. Dieterich Buxtehude (ca. 1637–1707), *Nun bitten wir den heiligen Geist*, BuxWV 208 (chorale prelude)

EDITION

Buxtehude's original notation for this piece was probably in the form of an organ tablature, in which notes and rhythms are indicated by letters and other symbols, without staff lines. The modern edition is based on an eighteenth-century manuscript in score notation, and the editor has distributed the notes onto three staves. The top staff is for the right hand, playing the decorated chorale cantus firmus on a solo manual; the middle staff is for the left hand, playing the two inner voices on a quieter accompanimental manual; and the feet play the bass, notated on the bottom staff, on the pedals.

PERFORMANCE ISSUES

The chorale text is a prayer for deliverance and redemption (see Ex. 11.1 in the main text), suggesting a quiet registration overall. Each of the three staves in the modern score would have been played on a separate keyboard with its own registration: a prominent soprano melody, quiet inner voices, and a distinct bass line. Although this score employs several French ornament signs, it is uncertain precisely how a German Baroque organist would have realized these signs or whether other contemporary French conventions, such as *notes inégales*, would have been applied. Fingering and pedal technique were probably quite different from those used today; in particular, Baroque organists rarely used the heels of the feet, confining their pedal technique to the toes and therefore using a primarily nonlegato type of articulation.

SOURCE

The edition reproduced here is from *Dietrich Buxtehude: Werke für Orgel*, ed. Philipp Spitta, rev. Max Seiffert, vol. 2 (Leipzig: Breitkopf und Härtel, 1904); it is based on a manuscript copy by the German organist-composer Johann Gottfried Walther (1684–1748).[29]

---

[29]Berlin, Staatsbibliothek, Mus. ms. 22541/3.

27. Dieterich Buxtehude (ca. 1637–1707), Praeludium in A minor, BuxWV 153

EDITION

Like Selection 26, this work probably was first notated in tablature, but in the absence of surviving seventeenth-century manuscripts it has been edited from an eighteenth-century copy in staff notation. The latter employs just two staves, including the pedal part as the lowest voice on the bottom staff. This edition, like most modern editions of organ music, sets the bass apart on its own staff.

PERFORMANCE ISSUES

A *praeludium* was traditionally played *cum organo pleno*, that is, using the full resources of the German Baroque organ to produce a massive sound. Contrast might have been produced by lightening the registration for one or more sections (e.g., the second fugue, mm. 67–104), but Baroque organs did not permit the frequent changes of timbre or dynamic level that are possible on many later instruments, nor does the music require them.

SOURCE

The edition reproduced here is from Dietrich Buxtehude, *Werke für Orgel*, ed. Philipp Spitta, rev. Max Seiffert, vol. 1 (Leipzig, Germany: Breitkopf und Härtel, 1903); it is based on the eighteenth-century manuscript Berlin, Staatsbibliothek, Mus. ms. 2681.

28. Johann Sebastian Bach (1685–1750), Prelude and Fugue in G, BWV 860, from *The Well-Tempered Clavier*, Part 1

EDITION

This edition is based on Bach's autograph manuscript of 1722, which contains the entire first part of the *Well-Tempered Clavier*.[30] The manuscript is a so-called fair copy, meaning that Bach had copied it from an earlier manuscript (perhaps his original composing score) now lost. A dozen or more manuscript copies by other eighteenth-century musicians may also have derived from the lost older autograph; one of these preserved an earlier version of the prelude that is four measures shorter.[31]

The unusual position of the key signature in the upper staff reflects that in Bach's manuscript (where this staff uses soprano clef). In the prelude, the apparent conflict between the time signatures of the two staves is merely a shorthand for the notation of triplets: each eighth note in common time is worth three sixteenths in $\frac{24}{16}$.

PERFORMANCE ISSUES

Bach does not specify a keyboard instrument, and both prelude and fugue could be played on clavichord, harpsichord, piano, or even organ, although harpsichord was probably the composer's first choice. (Fortepianos existed at the time of the work's composition, but it is unlikely that Bach had yet seen an example of the new instrument.) The two hands cross somewhat awkwardly in the prelude, in measures 2–3. But this does not necessarily indicate the use of two keyboards, such as were present on some harpsichords.

Bach wrote the work primarily for study, and thus the prelude might often have been played separately from the fugue. Tempo and expressive character must be determined from the music; the lively style and brilliant figuration of both movements suggest quick tempos and, on the harpsichord, a strong (loud) registration throughout. An ornament table in the Little Notebook for Wilhelm Friedemann Bach provides an introductory guide to the ornament signs in the fugue, although other contemporary music and treatises furnish valuable suggestions as well (see Selection 29).

SOURCE

This edition is reproduced from *Joh. Seb. Bach's Clavierwerke*, vol. 3, *Das Wohltemperierte Clavier*, ed. Franz Kroll, *Johann Sebastian Bach's Werke* 14 (Leipzig, Germany: Bach-Gesellschaft, 1866), 52–56.

---

[30]Berlin, Staatsbibliothek, Mus. ms. Bach P 415.
[31]This earlier version lacks mm. 7b–8a and 14b–17a; it was found in the so-called Konwitschny manuscript, now lost but preserved on microfilm.

29. Jean Henry d'Anglebert (1628–1691), François Couperin (1668–1733), and Jean-Philippe Rameau (1683–1764), Extracts from ornament tables

ORNAMENT NAME	ORNAMENT SIGN AND REALIZATION		
	D'Anglebert (1689)	Rameau (1724)	Couperin (1716)

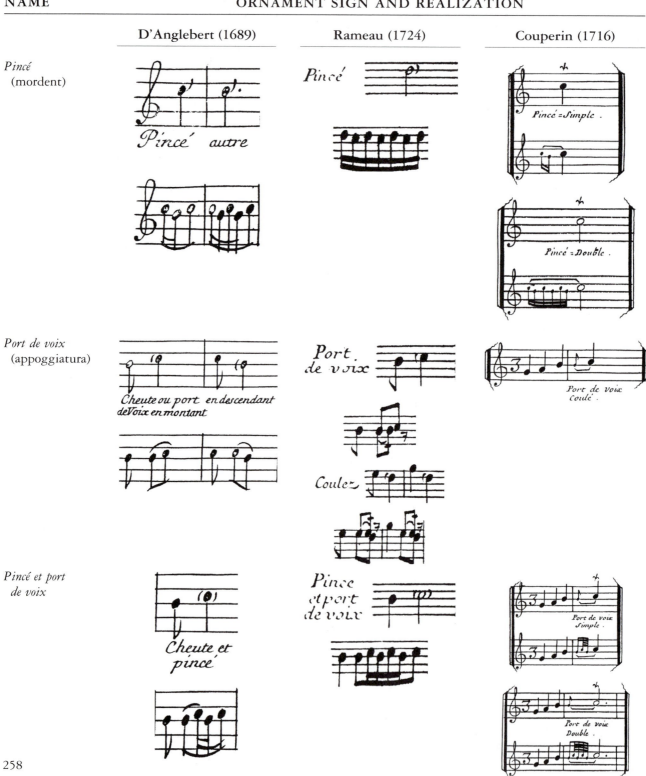

ORNAMENT
NAME   ORNAMENT SIGN AND REALIZATION

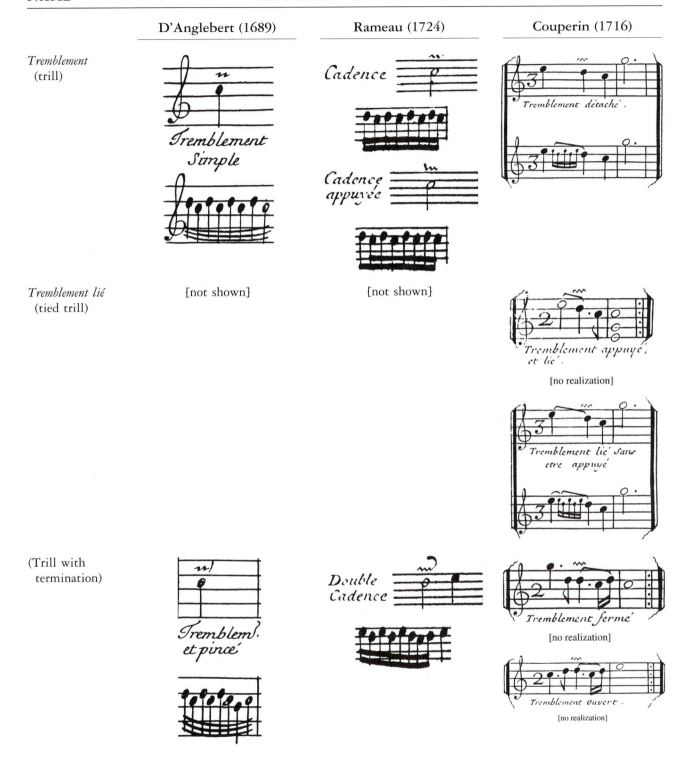

Tremblement
(trill)

Tremblement lié
(tied trill)

(Trill with
termination)

**ORNAMENT
NAME**

ORNAMENT SIGN AND REALIZATION

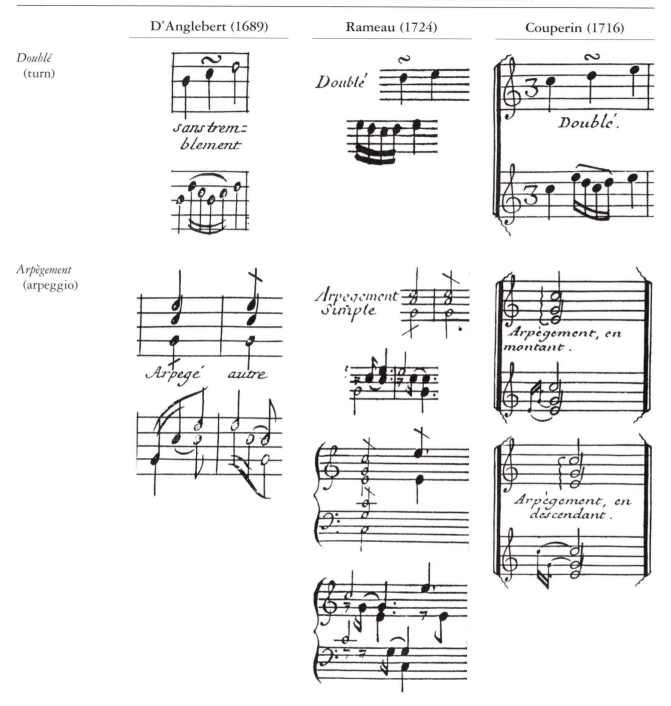

D'Anglebert (1689)   Rameau (1724)   Couperin (1716)

Doublé
(turn)

Arpègement
(arpeggio)

ORNAMENT NAME	ORNAMENT SIGN AND REALIZATION		
	D'Anglebert (1689)	Rameau (1724)	Couperin (1716)

Coulé (acciaccatura)

Détaché, coupé, aspiration (staccato)

PERFORMANCE ISSUES

Detailed attention to ornaments was typical of Baroque performance in general, but it was especially cultivated in France. Keyboard music tended to be particularly precise in the notation of ornamentation through symbols, but the same ornaments were used by all musicians, including singers.

These extracts are from the ornament tables that were included in three published collections of French Baroque harpsichord pieces. Each shows both the ornament sign and its performance or realization. Probably none of the realizations should be taken literally. The somewhat different signs, names, and realizations for each ornament given by these three French composers suggest that what is shown in each case is only a suggestion of what a good musician might have actually played. Certain common principles are nevertheless apparent. For example, trills normally start on the upper note, not the main one, and most ornaments seem to start on the beat.

SOURCES

The examples are reproduced from d'Anglebert's *Pièces de clavecin* (Paris, 1689), Rameau's *Pièces de clavessin* (Paris, 1724), and Couperin's *Pièces de clavecin . . . Premier livre* (Paris, 1713).[32] Rameau's work was published after Couperin's, but his ornament signs are illustrated in the middle column because of their closer similarity to those of d'Anglebert in column 1.

---

[32]All have been published in facsimile (New York: Broude).

30. François Couperin (1668–1733), *Vingt-unième ordre* (keyboard suite: selections)

a. *La reine des cœurs*

Lentement; et tres tendrement

b. *La Couperin*

D'une vivacité moderée

EDITION

This score has been newly prepared from the original printed edition. Modern clefs have been substituted and symbols for slurs modernized.

PERFORMANCE ISSUES

Unlike most of Bach's keyboard music, these pieces are unambiguously intended for the harpsichord—specifically the large, resonant French type of the early eighteenth century. A technique particularly idiomatic on such instruments is the so-called **overlegato**, whereby certain notes are held beyond their written lengths in order to blend together with the notes that follow. In some cases, Couperin indicates this through the use of extra stems on the noteheads (as in *La reine des cœurs*, left hand, mm. 3–7). Slurs can have the same meaning, as in *La Couperin*, measures 2 and 4.

Naturally, a performer must consider as well the many other conventions of the French style, including *notes inégales* and overdotting. Also notable here are Couperin's unusually precise tempo markings. It goes without saying that a player should also consult Couperin's ornament table (see Selection 29) as well as his treatise *L'art de toucher le clavecin* (The art of playing the harpsichord).[33]

Special concern for articulation and the proper grouping of notes is evident in the careful placement of slurs and in the breaking of beams for eighths and sixteenths at points where an articulation is intended (as in *La Couperin* after the first note of m. 7 in both hands). In the original, the slurs are drawn in a square form that resembles a bracket and thus perhaps encourages crisp articulation (see Fig. 11.1 in the text volume). This shape for the slur appears to be unique to Couperin, as is also true of two other signs: a large comma, used to indicate phrase divisions after weak beats and at other points where they might not be immediately obvious (see *La reine des cœurs*, m. 12; note that this division is in the right hand only); and a straight line occasionally used to connect two notes (as in *La reine des cœurs*, m. 1, bass), which appears to be identical in meaning to a slur.

SOURCE

This edition is based on Couperin's *Quatrième livre de pièces de clavecin* (Paris, 1730), which has been published in facsimile (New York: Broude, 1973).

---

[33]Paris, 1716; 2d ed., 1717; English trans. by Mevanwy Roberts as *The Art of Playing the Harpsichord* (Wiesbaden, Germany: Breitkopf und Härtel, 1961).

31. Salamone Rossi (?1570–ca. 1630), *Sonata sopra*
La Bergamasca

EDITION

The score has been newly prepared from a seventeenth-century edition consisting of separate partbooks. Small note values, originally separate, have been beamed together; barlines have been added and the rhythmic notation modernized (including the omission of a half rest at the beginning of each part in m. 1). The tied notation of the bass in measure 2 and elsewhere was a feature of some early continuo parts used to indicate the rhythmic placement of the second figure. Whether the slight clashes between the figures and the second part in measures 19, 23, and 27 were intended is uncertain.

PERFORMANCE ISSUES

Although Rossi did not specify the instrumentation of the upper parts, they are readily playable on violins. Wind instruments, of which the cornetto would have been the most likely early-Baroque alternative, would seem to be ruled out by the absence of pauses for breathing. The title of the original publication names the theorbo (chitarrone) as the bass instrument, but other instruments are possible, including Baroque guitar. The latter was often used in ostinato compositions, and Marini specified its use in the dances of his *Diversi generi di sonate*, op. 22 (Venice, 1655). However, the large continuo groups heard in some modern performances of this type of sonata, combining guitar, theorbo, harpsichord, and a bowed string instrument, are anachronistic. By the same token, the "country" style affected by some modern performers in playing this seemingly unsophisticated type of piece, although perhaps amusing, is unlikely to correspond with historical practice. Despite the possible origin of this type of music in improvisation, it remained a courtly genre cultivated by professional musicians.

SOURCE

The music is from *Il quarto libro de varie sonate, sinfonie . . . per sonar due violini et un chitarrone* (Venice, 1642; original edition: 1622).

32. Dario Castello (early 17th cent.), Sonata 12 from *Libro* II

EDITION

As in Selection 31, the score has been prepared from a seventeenth-century edition in separate partbooks. Barlines and beaming of small note values have been added and clefs and rhythmic notation modernized. In the source, the sextuplets in the solo passages (mm. 97ff.) are notated as thirty-seconds. Tempo marks do not always occur simultaneously in all parts, and, as in other early music printed from moveable type, it is often unclear exactly on which notes slurs and ornaments (the letter "t") are meant to appear. The edition reproduces the original placement of these indications as precisely as is practical. Accidentals and notes have been supplemented conservatively; such clashes as occur in measures 26 and 28 were evidently intended.

PERFORMANCE ISSUES

The upper parts are undesignated but must have been meant for violins or, more likely, cornettos, which produce an electrifying effect on the signal-like repeated notes of the opening subject. The original edition specifies the instrumentation of the third part as for *trombone* or *violetta*. The first instrument, probably the preferred choice, is similar to its modern equivalent, but it is uncertain what exactly was meant by *violetta*. The lowest note of this part is G, suggesting that it could have been played a type of small bass violin (*basso violetta da brazzo*) tuned an octave below the violin. The title page of the original edition indicates that the continuo part is for either organ or harpsichord.

The original parts contain significantly more performance indications than instrumental works published just a few years previously. Yet the exact meaning of these markings is rarely certain. Whether *presto* and *allegro* signify distinct tempos (as opposed to contrasting expressive characters) is unclear; even *adagio* may not indicate a slower actual beat than *allegro*, although in the solo passages it probably implies a degree of rhythmic freedom. The dynamic markings in measures 154–57 clearly denote echo effects between the two upper parts, but surely dynamics would be used elsewhere as well. The abbreviation "t" (as in m. 35) must mean *trillo* or *tremolo*, but it is not always clear on precisely which note the abbreviation is meant to appear; possibly it was understood as applying to all of the notes under the slur that usually accompanies it. Nor is it certain whether these words refer to a trill in the modern sense or to something resembling the vocal trillo, that is, a sort of intense vibrato. The latter seems to be written out in measures 33, 35, and elsewhere, but not in measures 96–97. The continuo part uses flats to signify minor chords, and sharps signify major chords, regardless of the actual notes called for (one natural sign does occur in the source, in the continuo part in m. 68, but the sign was not yet in general use).

SOURCE

The edition has been newly prepared from a facsimile of the second edition (Venice, 1644);[34] both the first edition (Venice, 1629) and the second edition bear the title *Sonate concertate in stil moderno: per sonar nel organo overo clavicembalo con diversi instrumenti a 1.2.3 e 4 voci: libro secondo*.

---

[34]Florence, Italy: Studio per Edizioni Scelte, 1981.

33. Biagio Marini (1594–1663), *Sonata variata* for violin and continuo

EDITION

Our score is based on the first edition, which included both a violin part and a score for the continuo player. Barlines, irregularly placed in the original, have been regularized to modern usage; time signatures have also been modernized, and beams have been added to small note values. The title appears simply as *Variata* in each of the original performing parts and as *per Sonar variate* in the table of contents. The changes of "key" signature at measures 16 and 87 are original, although they were understood as representing different transpositions of the Dorian or Aeolian mode rather than changes of tonality in the modern sense. The words *presto* and *Tardo* at measures 59 and 95, respectively, occur in the original score but may refer more to local changes of expressive character than to tempo as we understand it. *Tardo* (which seems to mean "ritard") might have been merely a warning not to execute the three eighth notes in measure 95 at the same speed as the preceding thirty-seconds.

PERFORMANCE ISSUES

This sonata was published as part of a large collection of instrumental music, much of it (including this work) suitable for performance as part of a church service as well as in domestic (chamber) settings. Hence organ as well as harpsichord or lute is a possible choice for the continuo instrument. The violin employed here was the early Baroque version of the modern instrument; Marini's music reveals sophisticated use of bowings, double stops, and high notes up to e''' (probably played in third position, with extension).

The style resembles that of a keyboard toccata in its frequent changes of character. Tempo changes are largely written into the music, as in the use of large note values at the beginning and much shorter ones in measures 8–12. It is uncertain whether the time signatures imply precise tempo relationships between the sections. In theory, the whole note of measures 1–38 is probably equal to the dotted whole note in the following measures, but Marini might have expected considerable freedom in this regard.

SOURCE

Our edition is based on Marini's *Sonate, sinfonie, canzoni, passemezzi, baletti, correnti, gagliarde, e retornelli per ogni sorte di instrumenti, opera ottava* (Venice: Magni, 1629), which is available in facsimile.[35]

---

[35]Florence: Studio per Edizioni Scelte, 2004. The 1629 edition was probably a reprint of one of 1626.

34. Heinrich Ignaz Franz Biber (1644–1704), Sonata 5 in E minor for violin and continuo (1681)

EDITION

The score has been prepared from a facsimile reprint of the first edition, a sumptuously engraved volume that includes a portrait showing the composer together with violin and spinet or virginal (hence suggesting a continuo instrument for the work). The first edition gives the music in score, and the present edition reproduces the latter with minimal alterations, chiefly the insertion of dotted barlines to conform with modern practice.

PERFORMANCE ISSUES

Biber specifies no particular continuo instrument, and the small harpsichord-type keyboard shown in his portrait is at best a suggestion of what might be used in this work. Organ and theorbo are other possibilities, although as in other seventeenth-century works the continuo "orchestras" heard in some modern performances are probably anachronistic.

By this date the abbreviation "t" in the violin part signified what we would call a trill, although unlike eighteenth-century trills these might have often started on the main note, not on the upper neighbor. Tempo marks are original, but whether *presto* is faster than *allegro* is uncertain. *Adagio* does not necessarily mean a very slow tempo, but it does imply rhythmic freedom, especially in the opening section.

A Baroque violinist would have approached the considerable technical challenges presented by this work in a somewhat different fashion from a modern player. For example, in the multiple stops of measures 109–11 and elsewhere, the lowest note was probably played on the beat, not before it; the second note from the bottom probably was played after the bottom note, not with it. Left-hand technique also differed, since the hand supported the instrument, which rested loosely on the shoulder and was not held in place by the chin. Obviously this did not prevent seventeenth-century players from shifting readily. Rhythmic freedom allowed them to take small amounts of time at leaps and other breaks in the melodic line; a series of steady thirty-seconds as in measures 11–13 would not have been played metronomically. Whether Biber expected players to add slurs is uncertain; he has marked a great many already, implying that he has marked all that are necessary.

SOURCE

The edition is based on Biber's *Sonatae violino solo* (Salzburg, 1681), which is available in a facsimile edition.[36]

---

[36]Edited by Manfred Hermann Schmid (Bad Reichenhall, Germany: Comes, 1991).

35. Giovanni Legrenzi (1626–90), Sonata *La Strasolda* for two violins and continuo, op. 2, no. 4

EDITION

The score has been newly prepared from the first edition. Although printed in separate parts, the original is otherwise close to modern notation. Small note values, originally all separate, have been beamed together, and a small number of barlines have been added; the notation of accidentals has been updated. In measure 50, a sharp on f′ in the second part has been deleted; in measure 90, the last note of the bass has been changed from B to G.

PERFORMANCE ISSUES

This work was probably heard in both secular and sacred contexts. It might have been played in church as a substitute for certain parts of the Roman Catholic liturgy, but it also was probably heard in concerts sponsored by learned academies (*accadamie*) and by private individuals, including the composer himself. Even private chamber performances might have used a small organ as the continuo instrument, although harpsichord and theorbo are also possibilities. In the original edition, this work occurs alongside other duo (SS and SB) and trio (SSB) sonatas. The present work is an SS duo sonata; hence the composer may have envisioned the violins being accompanied solely by a keyboard instrument, although it is possible that a cello or other bass instrument would have doubled the continuo. This, however, would have required the player to read the continuo part over the keyboard player's shoulder, for there was no separate printed part for *violone* as there is in the SB and SSB sonatas.

As in other seventeenth-century works, *presto* and *adagio* seem to be generic "fast" and "slow" markings, respectively, that do not signify the extremes that these words came to mean in later centuries. Time signatures probably still retained proportional significance, and the entire piece could be performed with each measure having approximately the same duration—that is, with the half note set at MM. = 60 in common-time sections, 90 in triple (in that case, the word *adagio* might be interpreted literally to mean a slight "easing" of the tempo). Extensive embellishment of the short adagio seems out of place.[37]

SOURCE

This edition is based on a microfilm copy of the original, *Sonate a due e tre di Giovanni Legrenzi . . . opera seconda* (Venice: Magni, 1655).

---

[37]For further discussion of performance issues, including the realization of the figured bass, see *The Instrumental Music of Giovanni Legrenzi: Sonate a due e tre Opus 2, 1655*, ed. Stephen Bonta (Cambridge, Mass.: Department of Music, Harvard University, distributed by Harvard University Press, 1984).

36. Arcangelo Corelli (1653–1713), Sonata in C for violin and continuo, op. 5, no. 3

EDITION

This is a nineteenth-century edition based on Corelli's original publication together with several of its numerous later reprints. The editor has combined the score published as the first edition with the embellished version of the violin part published by the Amsterdam printer Estienne Roger in 1710. The latter is shown on the staff labeled "Corelli's Graces," echoing Roger's claim that the embellishments were "composed by Corelli as he plays them."[38] The lowest staff, here labeled *cembalo e violone* (harpsichord and string bass), was originally designated *cembalo o violone* (harpsichord *or* string bass), leaving performers the option to perform the sonata as a duet for two string instruments, the lower one (most likely a cello) adding double stops where possible to fill in the harmony.

PERFORMANCE ISSUES

Roger gave embellishments only for the two slow movements, but it is likely that players added ornaments elsewhere as well. Roger claimed in a catalogue of works for sale that he possessed letters from the composer proving that these were Corelli's own embellishments. These documents do not survive, but even if Corelli did write the embellishments shown here, it is unlikely that he would have always played the same ones. Surely, most good players would have varied the embellishments from one performance to the next. Hence these "graces"—an old expression for "ornaments"—were probably intended to serve primarily as models for inexperienced players to imitate.

As in Biber's music, chords of three or four notes (as in third movement, mm. 17–18) were probably executed by placing the lowest note on the beat, not before it; the bow was probably drawn over the strings smoothly, without holding out the lower notes in a momentary double stop (as in modern technique). Unfortunately, Roger did not indicate how the violinist is to play the passage at the close of the second movement, marked *Arpeggio* (mm. 46–50). Some sort of rapidly broken chords was apparently intended, despite the notation with ties (which misleadingly suggests sustained notes).

SOURCES

Our edition is reproduced from *Les œuvres de Arcangelo Corelli*, ed. J. Joachim and F. Chrysander, 5 vols. (London: Augener, 1888–91), 3:26–35. The original edition was entitled *Sonate a violino e violono o cimbalo* (Rome: Pietra Santa, 1700).[39]

---

[38]The title of Roger's edition reads: *Sonate a violino e violone o cimbalo . . . Troisieme edition ou l'on a joint les agremens des Adagio de cet ouvrage, composez par Mr. A. Corelli comme il les joue* (Amsterdam: Roger, 1710). For a facsimile, see Arcangelo Corelli, *Sonate a violino e violone o cimbalo*, ed. Marcello Castellani, Archivum musicum 21 (Florence: Studio per Edizione Scelte, 1979).
[39]A facsimile of the first edition is published alongside the facsimile of the embellished edition by Roger; see previous note.

37. Giuseppe Torelli (1658–1709), Sinfonia in D for trumpet, strings, and continuo, G. 8

EDITION

This work was composed for the large orchestral forces available at the church of San Petronio in Bologna. The four lower parts (two violins, viola, and continuo) were intended for multiple players, most of whom were ripieno players who rested in certain passages for soloists. In this score, pauses by the ripieno players are marked by the abbreviations "−ripieno" in the violin parts and "−bs. spezzato" in the continuo part. The latter refers to the *basso spezzato*, evidently a ripieno part for an additional bass instrument, possibly playing at double-bass pitch. Although the term *violone* today means double bass, the violone part in this score is probably for an instrument at regular pitch, playable by a second cello.

PERFORMANCE ISSUES

In addition to the instrument considerations mentioned above, the trumpet part is for a "natural" instrument without valves, and the continuo was furnished explicitly by an organ. To what degree the soloist would have embellished the trumpet part is uncertain, but all players would certainly have added customary cadential trills and other ornaments. On the other hand, the staccato strokes in the adagio not only imply detached performance but discourage the addition of any embellishment. As in other seventeenth-century works, the word *adagio* probably does not indicate a particularly slow tempo.

SOURCE

The work is preserved in manuscript parts in Bologna, Basilica di San Petronio, Archivio Musicale, D. VI. 2.

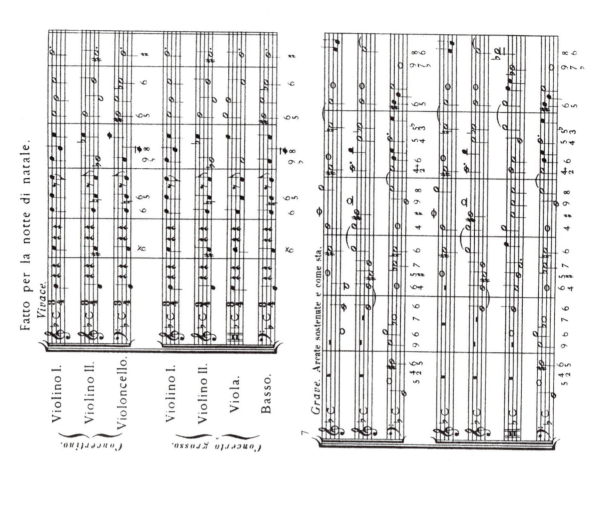

38. Arcangelo Corelli (1653–1713), Concerto grosso in G minor, op. 6, no. 8, "Christmas"

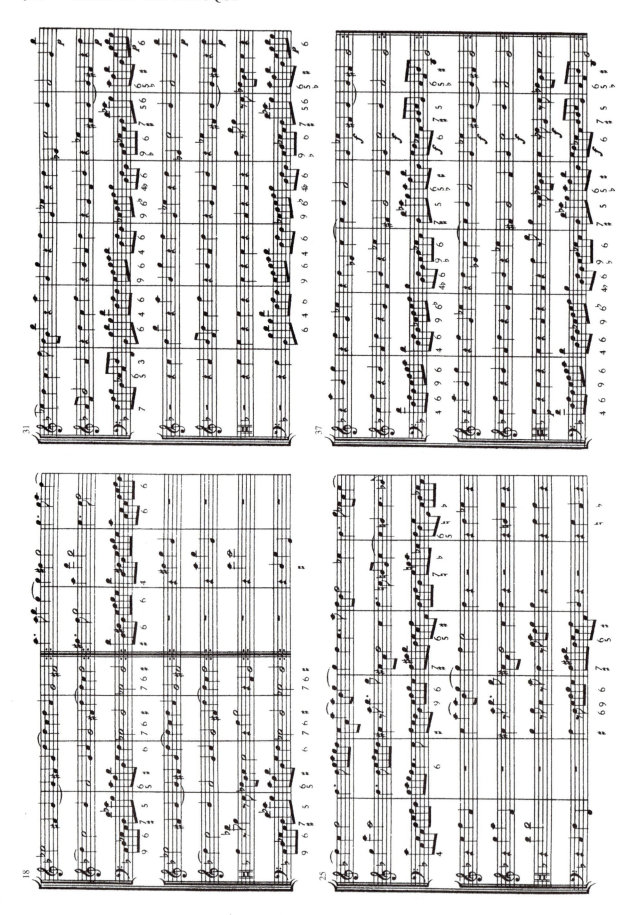

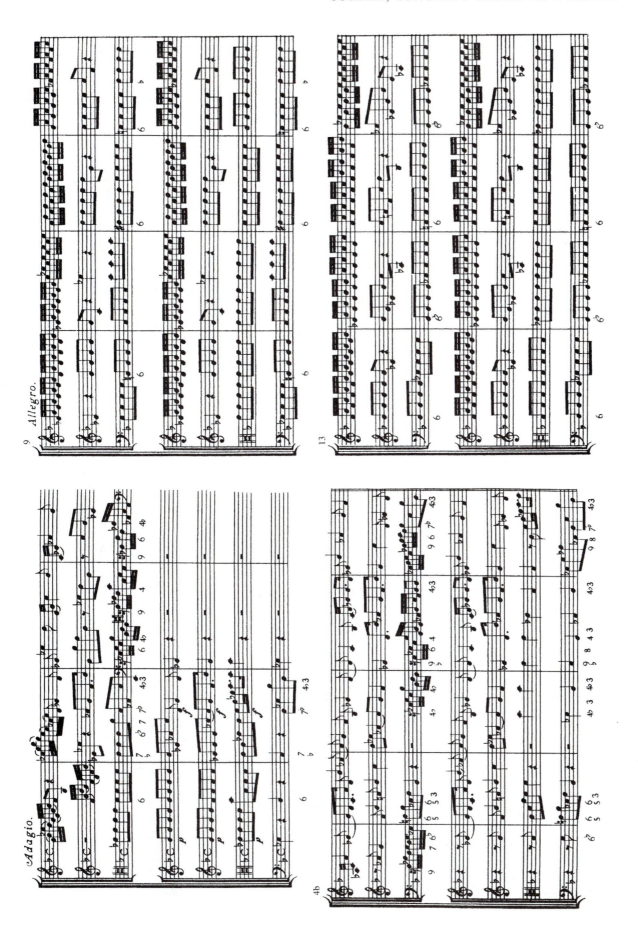

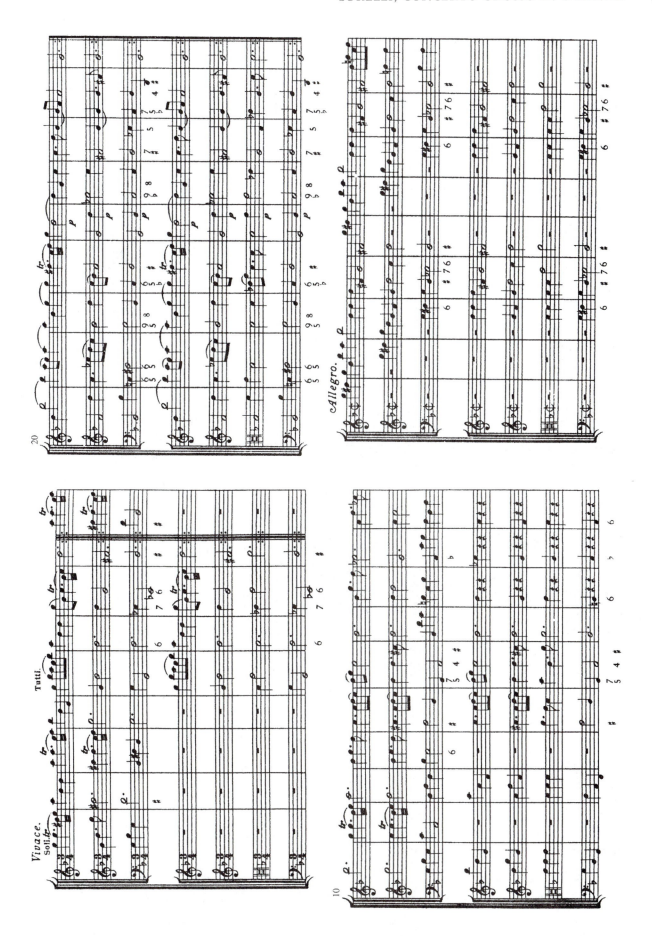

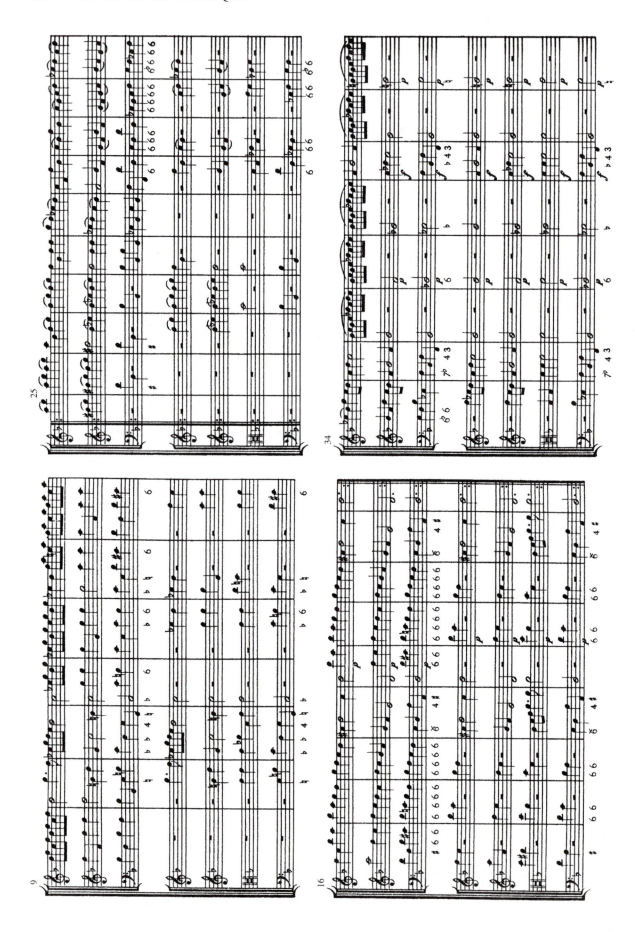

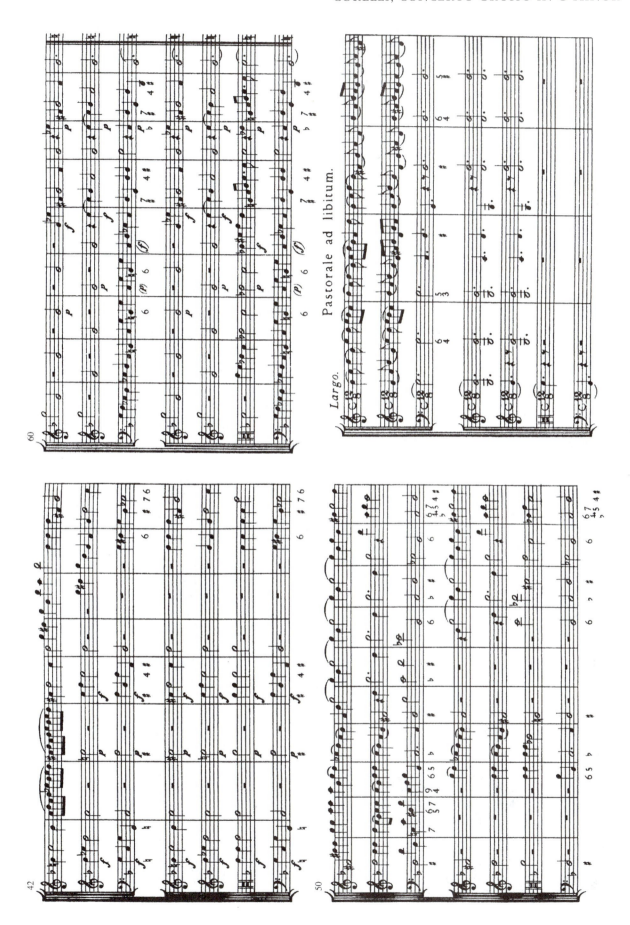

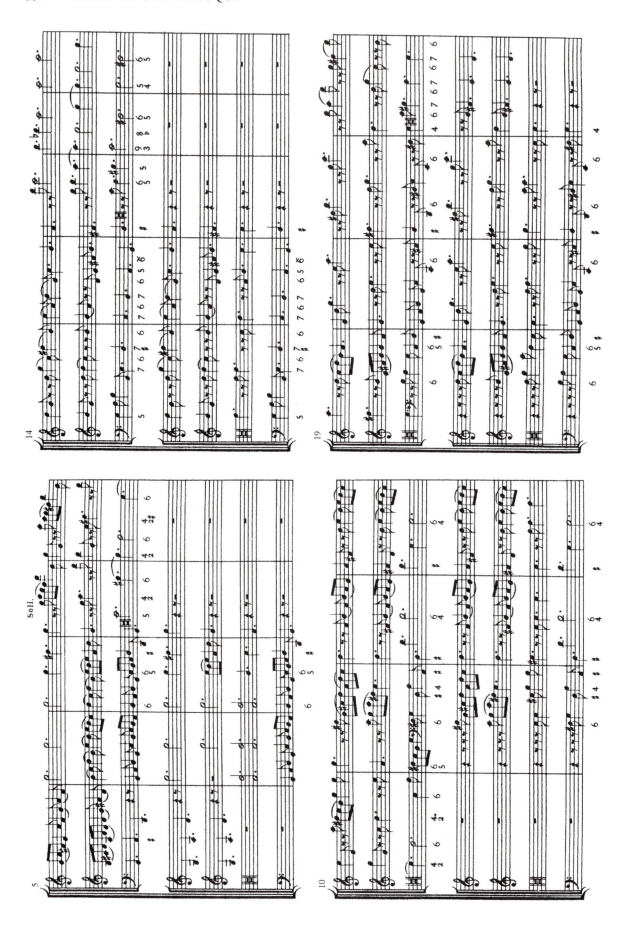

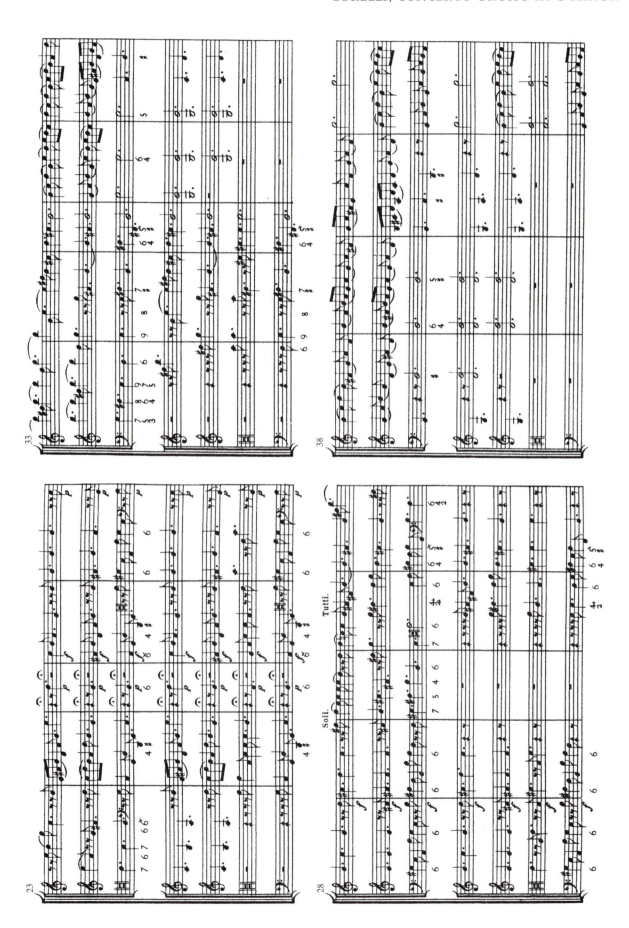

EDITION

As for selection 36, our score is from the nineteenth-century edition of Corelli's works, based on eighteenth-century editions of his Opus 6 concertos. The work was originally published in a set of seven individual partbooks. The layout of our score, with the solo parts at the top, is editorial; in Corelli's manuscript, all four violin parts are at the top, with the viola, solo cello, and *basso* (continuo) parts beneath, in that order.[40]

The opening textual rubric, *Fatto per la notte di natale*, means "written for Christmas Eve"; whether it is accurate is unknown. At measure 7, *arcate sostenute e come sta* means "with sustained bows, as it is"—that is, without improvised embellishment. The absence of similar markings elsewhere implies that soloists would have felt free to embellish, especially in the Da Capo section of the adagio (mm. 22–29). The last movement is headed *Pastorale ad libitum*, meaning that this closing dance can be omitted if one likes. This might be because it was a later addition or because it was intended particularly for performances at Christmas.

PERFORMANCE ISSUES

As a sort of expanded trio sonata, this work can be performed satisfactorily without the ripieno parts (labeled "concerto grosso" in our score). The figures in the part labeled "violoncello" imply a keyboard realization, but the part was unfigured in Corelli's score and may have been originally meant for cello alone. The preferred keyboard instrument for the ripieno basso continuo part was perhaps organ, especially if the work was indeed intended for use as a church concerto for Christmas Eve.

The ripieno string parts might be performed by a string quartet—one player to a part. But at least one contemporary account reports the performance of this type of music by large ensembles, with multiple players for both the *concertino* and *concerto grosso*. Any such large-scale performance would include at least one double-bass instrument doubling the ripieno bass part.

SOURCE

The score is reproduced from *Les œuvres de Arcangelo Corelli*, ed. J. Joachim and F. Chrysander (London: Augener, 1888–91), 5:150–70. The first edition was entitled *12 Concerti Grossi* (Amsterdam: Roger, 1714).

---

[40]Facsimile of the autograph score of the concluding *Pastorale* in Arcangelo Corelli, *Gesamtausgabe*, vol. 4, ed. Rudolf Bossard (Cologne: Arno Volk, 1978). Corelli's manuscript for the remaining movements does not survive.

39. Antonio Vivaldi (1678–1741), Concerto in E for violin, strings, and continuo, op. 3, no. 12 (R. 265)

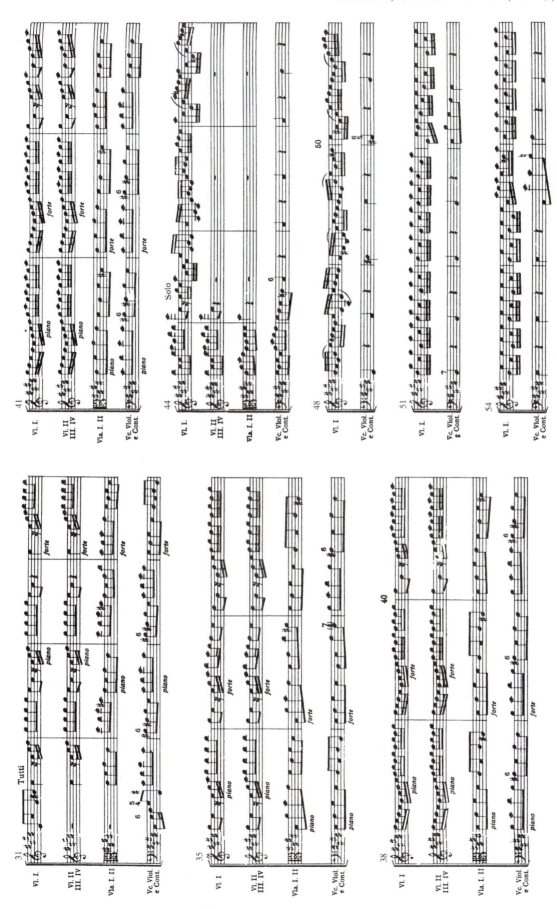

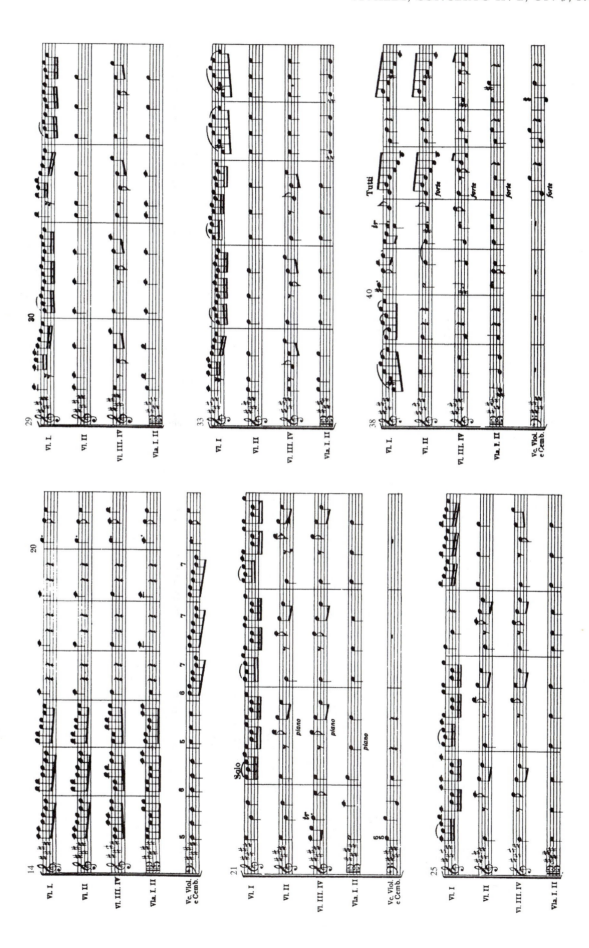

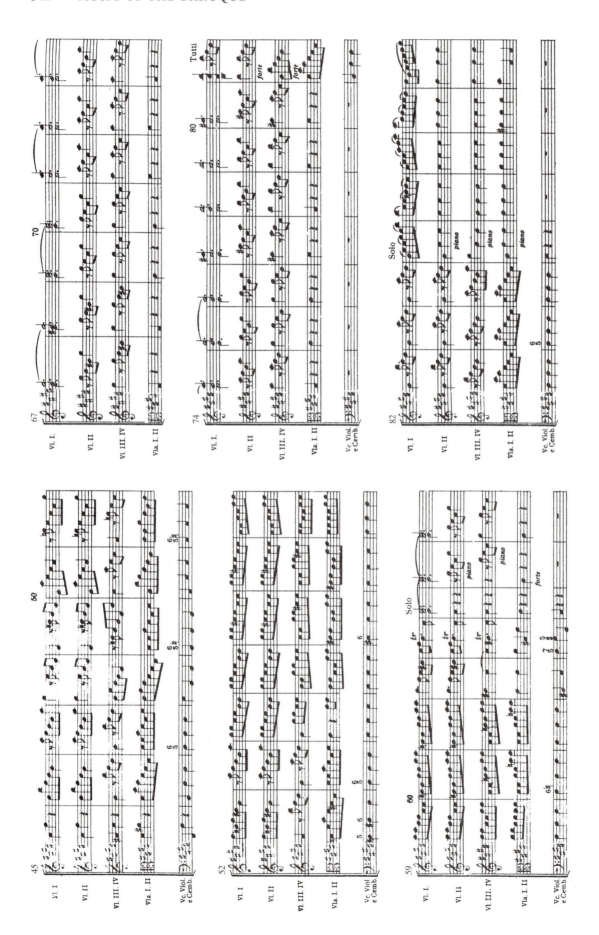

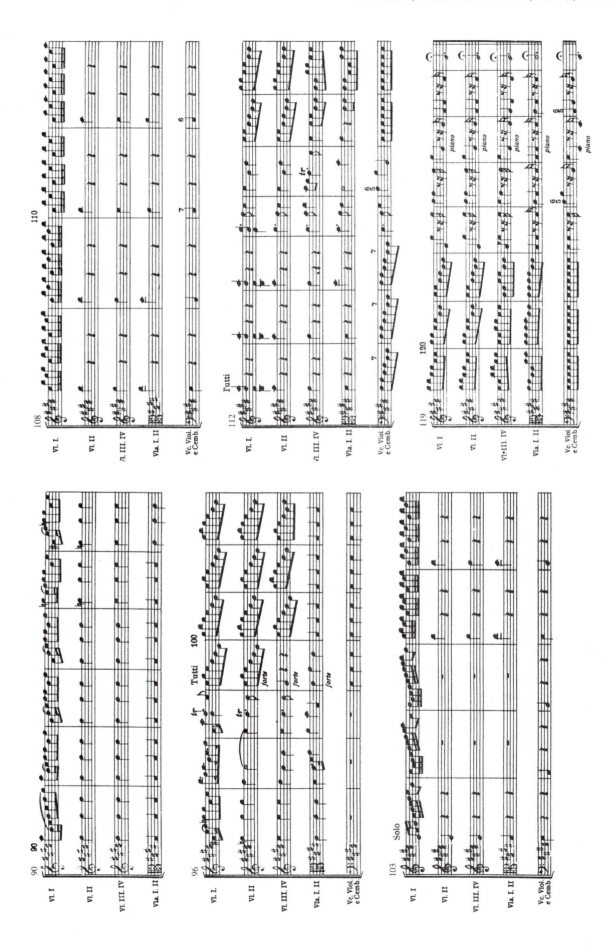

EDITION

Our score is reproduced from a pre–World War II edition based on the eight partbooks that constituted the early editions of Vivaldi's Opus 3. The part labels reflect this, naming four violin parts and two viola parts. But the present work is, in effect, a concerto for one solo violin, two ripieno violins, viola, and continuo. The part designated as the second violin functions as the first ripieno violin, and the third and fourth violins (whose parts are identical) function as the second ripieno part. The two viola parts are also identical, as are the two bass parts.

PERFORMANCE ISSUES

From the publication of Opus 3 in eight partbooks, it is doubtful whether Vivaldi intended any doubling of the parts (beyond that mentioned above) except for the violone and keyboard continuo. The words *solo* and *tutti* in various passages in the first violin part serve merely to alert the player to the presence or absence of the ripieno parts of these points.

As in any Italian Baroque concerto, the soloist might well add embellishment, especially in the second movement. The apparent double and triple stops in the first movement (mm. 58–65) were surely meant to be broken in sixteenth notes, following the pattern of the preceding measures. Similarly, in one passage in the third movement, the solo part is notated as sustained chords (mm. 64–80) but is presumably meant to be played as arpeggios (compare the end of Selection 36, second movement).

SOURCE

This edition by Heinrich Husmann (Zürich: Eulenburg, 1939) is based on Vivaldi's *L'estro armonico* (Amsterdam: Roger, 1711; numerous reprints).

40. Johann Sebastian Bach (1685–1750),
Brandenburg Concerto no. 2 in F, BWV 1047

CONCERTO II.

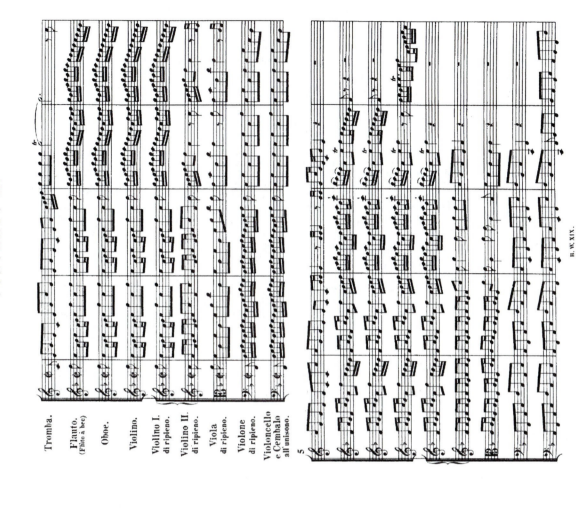

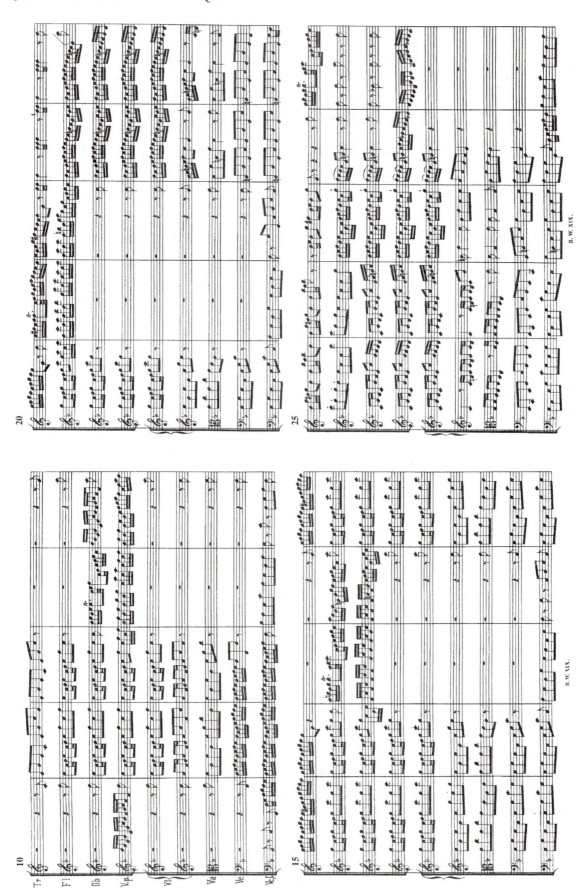

B.W. XIX.

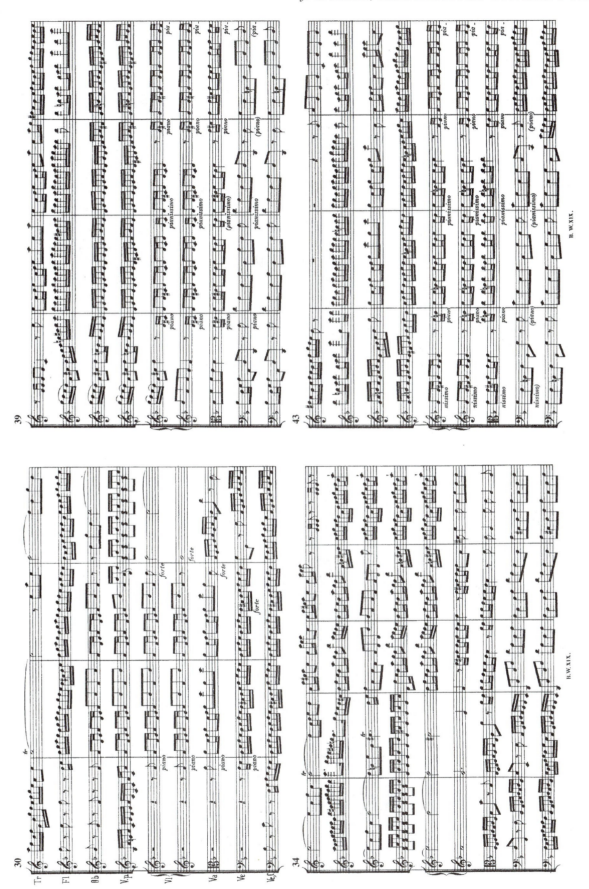

B. W. XII.

B. W. XIX.

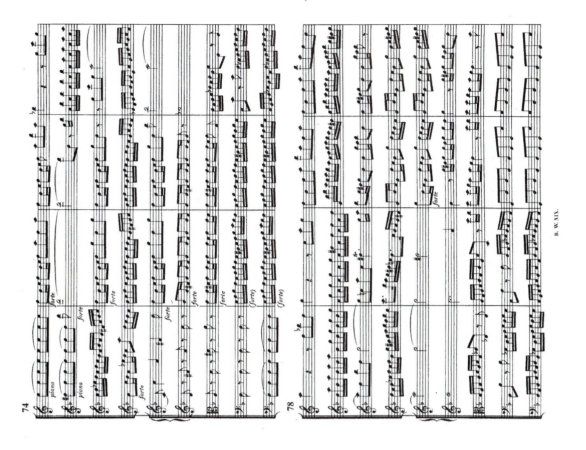

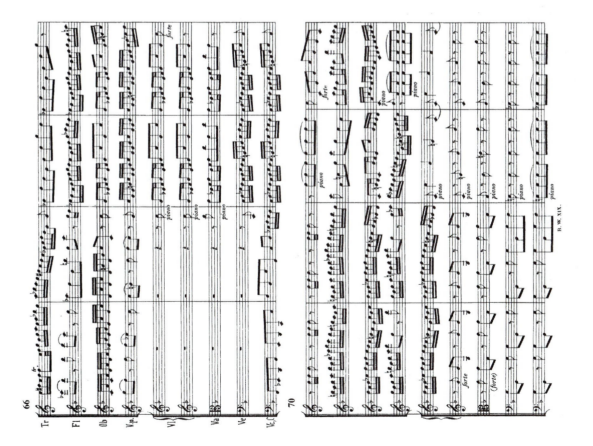

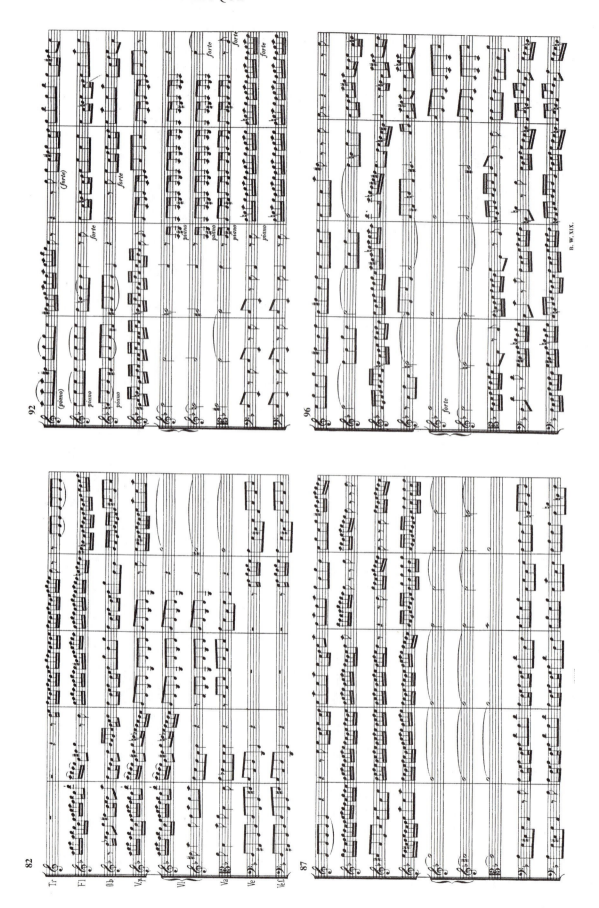

B. W. XIX.

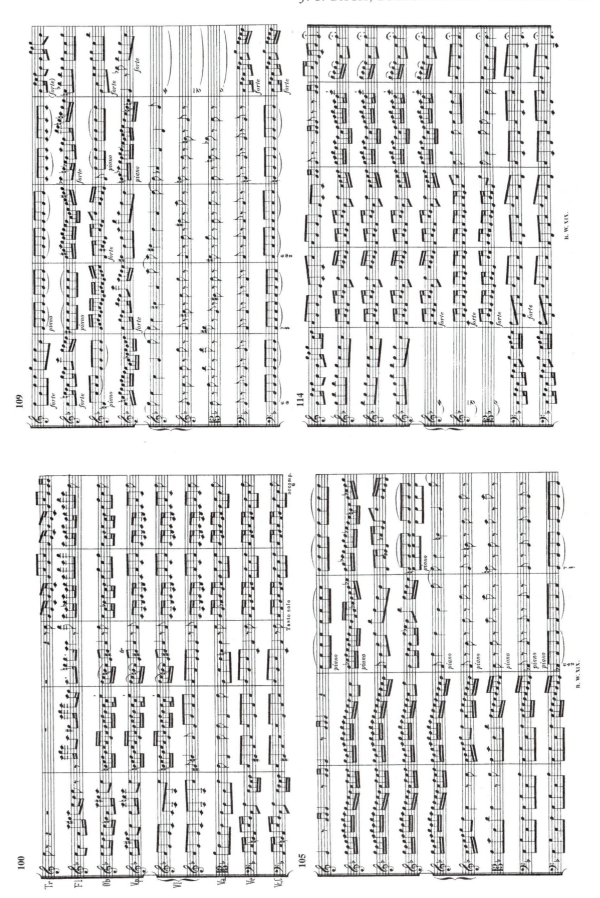

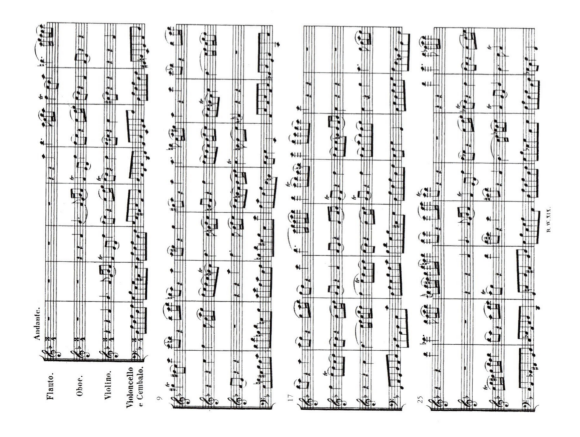

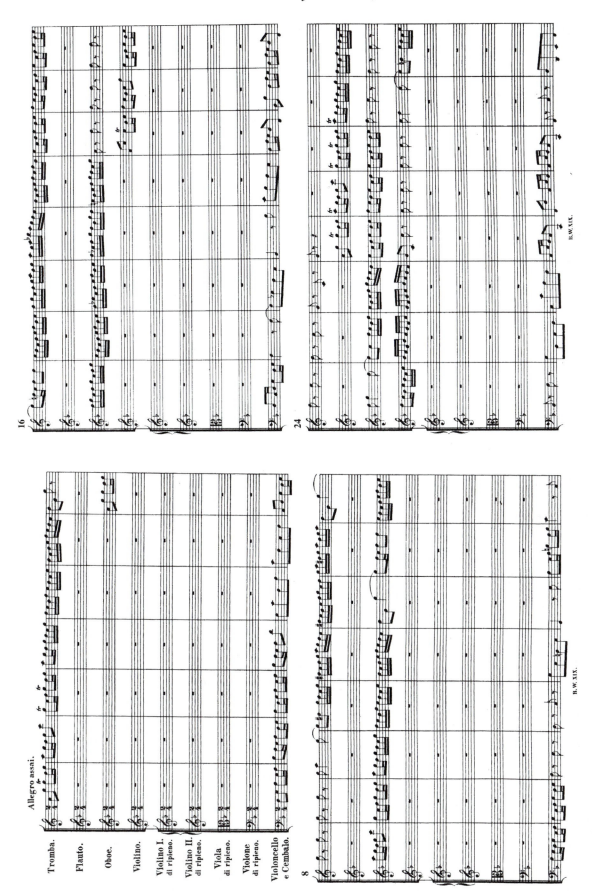

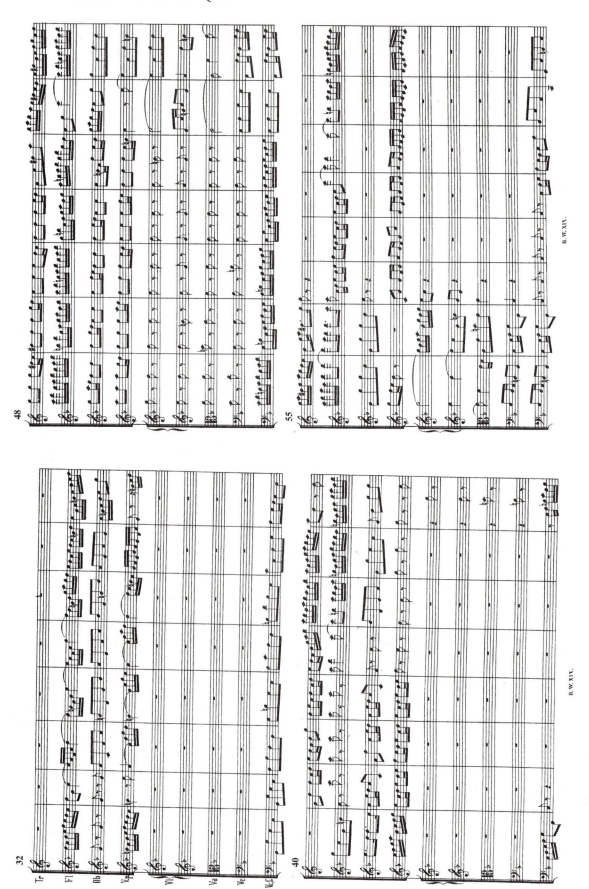

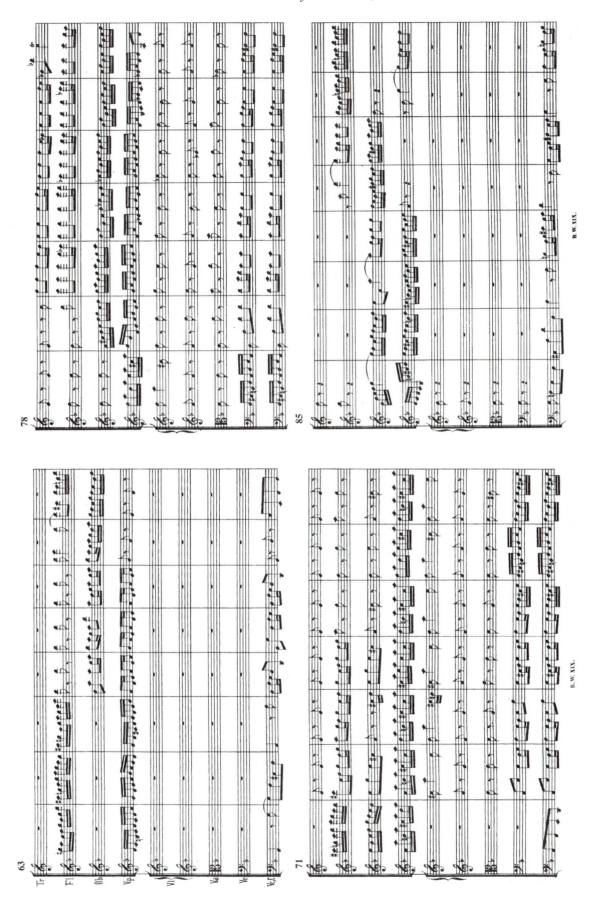

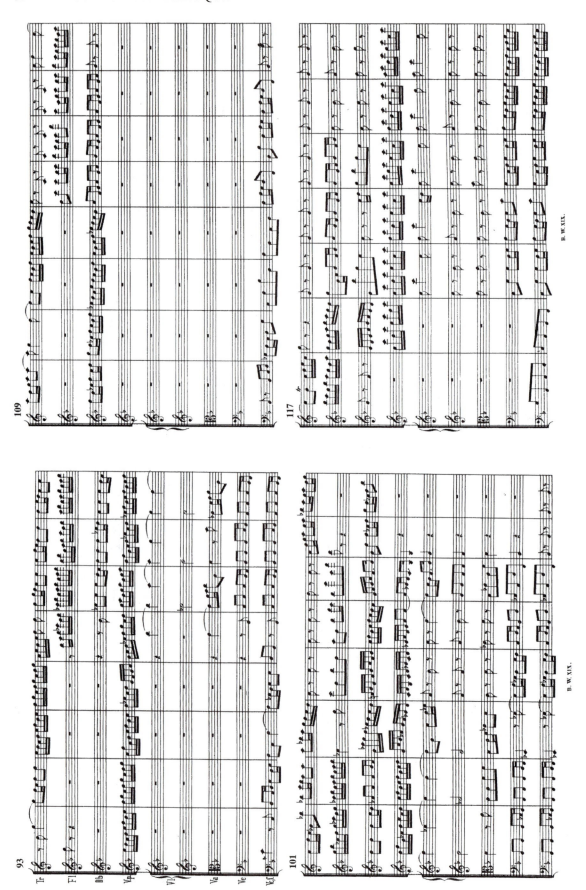

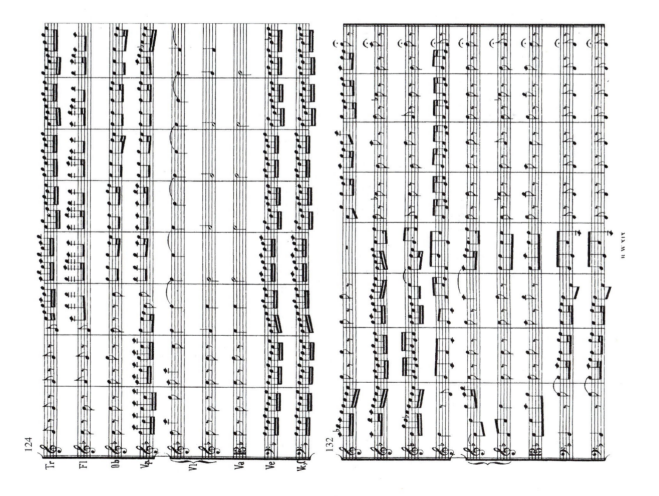

EDITION

This score is from the nineteenth-century complete edition of Bach's works. It is based closely on Bach's autograph manuscript score of the six concertos, which he presented in 1721 to the margrave of Brandenburg-Schwedt. Bach's manuscript is unusual in its careful listing of the instruments, including the specification of ripieno parts. Nevertheless it is incomplete for performance purposes, for the continuo lacks the figures that Bach often notated only in the individual part after it was copied from his score.

The part labels of our score, adapted from Bach's, can be understood as follows: trumpet; recorder; oboe; principal or solo violin; first and second ripieno violins; ripieno viola; ripieno bass instrument—possibly a bass violin or a large viola da gamba sounding at written pitch; and cello and harpsichord, doubling one another at the unison.

PERFORMANCE ISSUES

Like Selection 38, this work was very likely intended for performance with a single player on each part; moreover, it could be performed without the ripieno parts.[41] The trumpet has a transposing part, notated in C but sounding a fourth higher. Today, players often use the so-called Bach or "piccolo" trumpet, a small version of the modern valved trumpet. But Bach's trumpet was a "natural" brass instrument lacking valves, and its somewhat mellower tone and smaller volume are less likely to overbalance the much quieter recorder.

SOURCE

Our edition is based on Bach's autograph score in Berlin, Staatsbibliothek, Amalienbibliothek ms. 78.

---

[41] An edition has been published in this form, including as well a few alternative readings found in early manuscript copies: see Johann Sebastian Bach, *Concerto da camera F-dur*, ed. Klaus Hofmann (Kassel, Germany: Bärenreiter, 1998).

41. Georg Philipp Telemann (1681–1767), *Nouveau quatutor* no. 6 in E minor for flute, violin, viola da gamba (or cello) and continuo, TWV 43:e4 (first, second, fifth, and sixth movements

Prélude

359

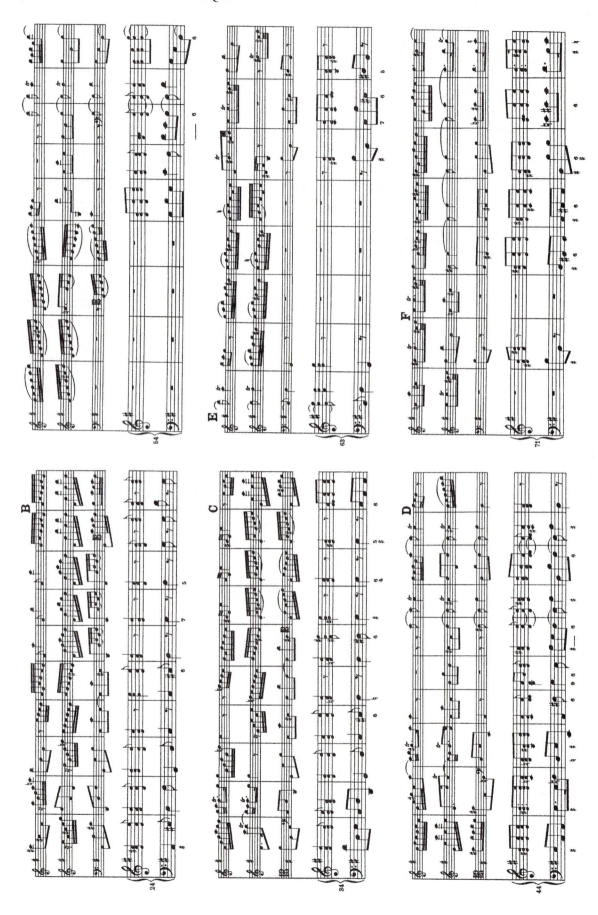

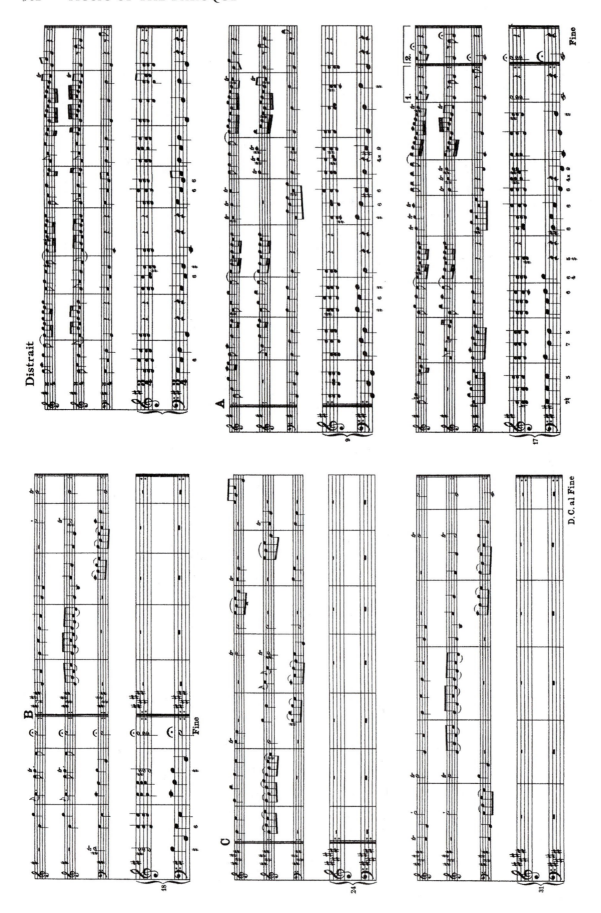

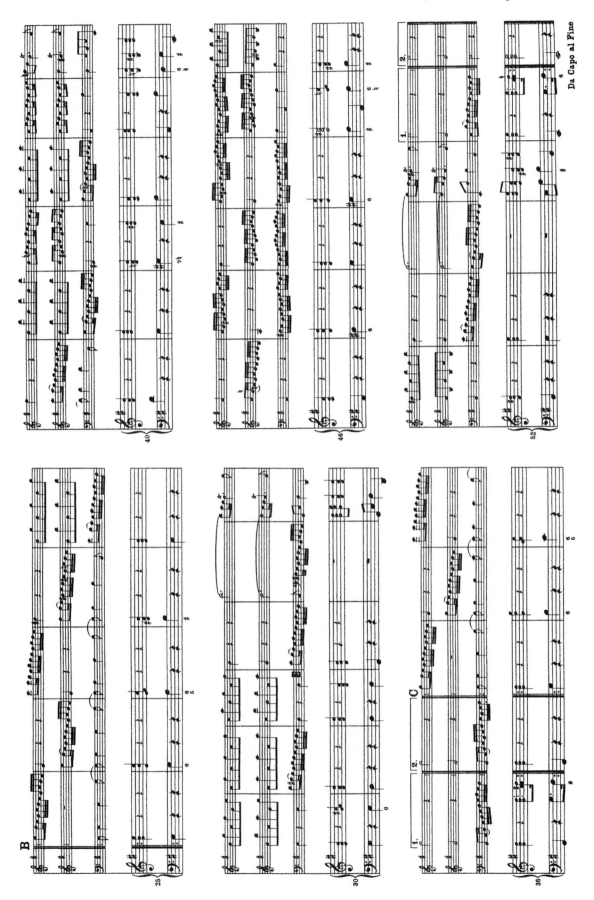

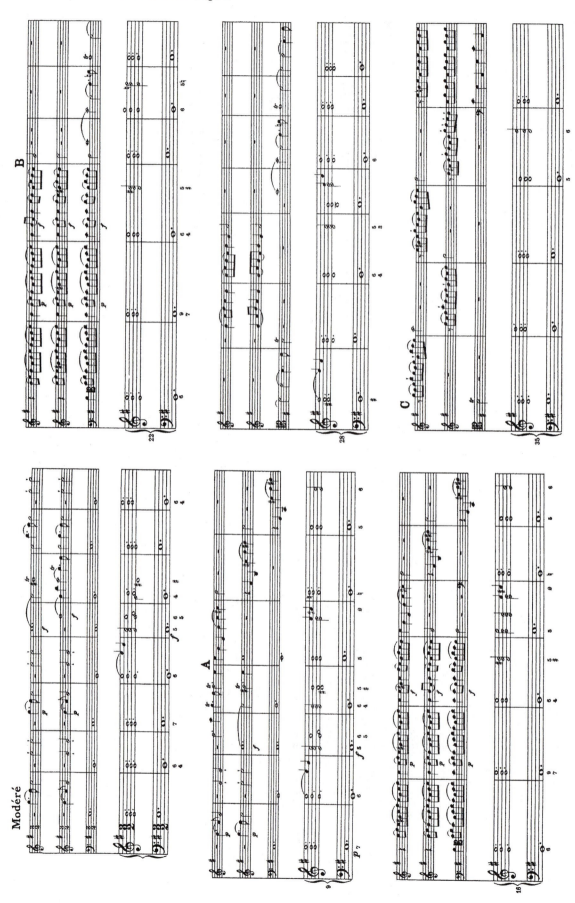

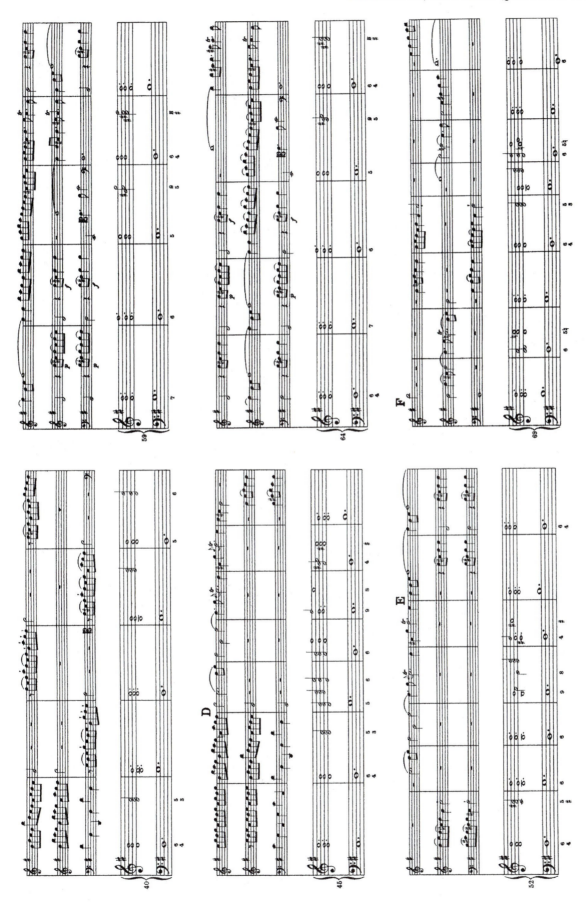

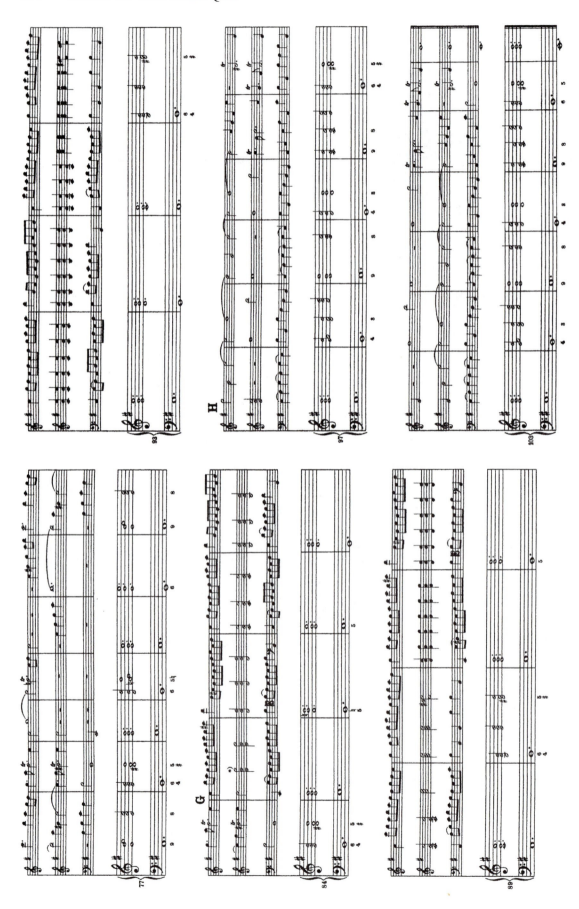

EDITION

This pre–World War II score was intended to serve as a keyboard part. Thus it includes an editorial realization of the figured bass, and the three melody parts are printed in small notes. The rehearsal letters (the large "A," "B," and so forth) are also editorial. Otherwise, it is an accurate transcription of the original publication in separate parts, although it omits the part for viola da gamba (see below).

PERFORMANCE ISSUES

The individual parts of Telemann's first edition included both the original viola da gamba part and the composer's adaptation of it for the cello; either could be used as the lowest of the three melody parts. Telemann and his contemporaries often gave players such options, thus making compositions available to performers who lacked one instrument or the other.[42]

The figured bass realization is appropriately simple in style. But like many realizations published during the twentieth century, it errs in rising too high, often crossing above the highest melody part or doubling it. Moreover, the steady three-part chords of the right hand would sound clunky and dull if played as written. A good player will improvise a lower and more flexible part, arpeggiating many of the chords and varying the number of voices.

SOURCE

This score is based on the first edition, *Nouveaux quatuors en six suites* (Paris, 1738).[43]

---

[42]For the viola da gamba part, see the facsimile edition listed below or the edition in Georg Philipp Telemann, *Musikalische Werke*, vol. 19, *Zwölf Pariser Quartette Nr. 7–12*, ed. Walter Bergmann (Kassel, Germany: Bärenreiter, 1965), 133–55.

[43]A facsimile (in separate partbooks) is published by Performers' Facsimiles (New York, 1998). The present score is reproduced from Georg Philipp Telemann, *Quartett in e-moll*, ed. Ellinor Dohrn, Nagels Musik-Archiv 10 (Hanover, Germany: Nagel, 1928).

42. Carl Philipp Emanuel Bach (1714–1788), "Württemberg" Sonata no. 1 in A minor for keyboard, W. 49/1

EDITION

This score is a close transcription of the original edition, which was printed with unusual care. Perhaps the only anomaly from the standpoint of modern notation is the unmarked switch to $\frac{2}{4}$ meter at measure 20 of the first movement (both first and second endings). Similar changes of meter occur occasionally in other works of C. P. E. Bach.

PERFORMANCE ISSUES

Many performance questions arising in this work are addressed in the composer's *Essay on the True Manner of Playing Keyboard Instruments*, whose first volume was published nine years after the present sonata.[44] Much can also be learned from the nearly contemporary treatise on flute performance by Bach's Berlin colleague Quantz.[45] Quantz's treatise goes far beyond the flute, including detailed instructions on the performance of ornaments and the interpretation of tempo marks.

Yet neither book answers the most fundamental question arising in this piece: For what instrument did Bach intend it? The Italian term *cembalo* used in the original title could at this date refer to any stringed keyboard instrument: harpsichord, clavichord, or the new fortepiano. The last was still extremely rare in 1742, when this sonata was written. Nine years later, in his *Essay*, Bach described the clavichord as the instrument "on which a player is best judged," implying that it was the most demanding and the best for practice. Solo sonatas such as this one would have been meant primarily for private playing, and although this sonata contains only two dynamic levels—*piano* and *forte*, obtainable on the two manuals (keyboards) of a large harpsichord—others in the set also call for *pianissimo*, suggesting use of the clavichord. On the other hand, the brilliant style of the outer movements of this work would be especially effective on the harpsichord.

Smaller puzzles in this work include the interpretation of the dotted rhythm in measure 4 of the first movement, where the vertical allignment of the notes suggests that the eighths in the lower voices should be "double dotted," making the following sixteenths simultaneous with the thirty-seconds in the upper voice. In measures 24–25 the notes are alligned differently, but perhaps this was an oversight.

The *Essay* answers many questions concerning the interpretation of ornament signs and other symbols. But in 1742 the composer was not yet using all of the signs described in his later treatise. Hence the abbreviation *tr* (for "trill") must be interpreted in various ways, corresponding to different versions of the trill and perhaps other ornaments (such as the turn) that would later be indicated by different signs. In the first movement, the trills in measure 13 might be short—even abbreviated to a single note, that is, an upper neighbor played as an appoggiatura, if the player cannot play even a short trill in the time available. But at the end of the slow movement one would intrepret *tr* as a long trill, concluding with a turn. What all trills have in common in Bach's works—but not necessarily those of all his contemporaries—is that they start on the upper note, played on the beat.

This is among the composer's earliest works in which the written values of some small notes—appoggiaturas, as in measure 7 of the last movement—were meant to indicate their actual rhythm in performance. Yet the *Essay* distinguishes between "variable" and

---

[44] *Versuch über die wahrer Art das Clavier zu spielen* (Berlin, 1753–62); English translation by William J. Mitchell as *The True Art of Playing Keyboard Instruments* (New York: Norton, 1949).

[45] *Versuch einer Anweisung das Flöte traversiere zu spielen* (Berlin, 1752; facsimile, Kassel, Germany: Bärenreiter, 2000); English translation by Edward R. Reilly as *Essay on Playing the Flute*, reissue of the 2d edition (Boston: Northeastern University Press, 2001).

"invariable" appoggiaturas, that is, of definite and indefinite value. The letter type, as in measure 10 of the first movement, might be played very short.

The fermata in the second-to-last measure of the second movement indicates a cadenza, as described in the text volume. Simple cadenzas might also have been played at the fermatas found earlier in this movement, where the word *adagio* indicates a ritard and perhaps also suggests some sort of embellishment. Melodic embellishment or variation might also have been applied to the theme when it returns at measures 21 and 33.

In the quick movements, the repeats were not regarded as optional, as they often are today. On the contrary, they provided players with an opportunity to improvise variations, just as in the repeated A section of a da capo aria. Bach would publish a number of sonatas in which the repeats are written out with embellishments (so-called varied reprises). He also left behind many examples of written-out cadenzas; below is one possibility for the slow movement.[46]

SOURCE

This score has been prepared from the original edition, *Sei sonate per cembalo . . . Opera seconda* (Nuremberg, Germany: Haffner, 1744), which is available in facsimile.[47]

[46]This cadenza was originally a third higher, in C major; it was intended for the slow movement of the Concerto in E minor for keyboard and strings, W. 24.
[47]*The Collected Works for Solo Keyboard by Carl Philipp Emanuel Bach*, 6 vols., edited with introductions by Darrell Berg (New York: Garland, 1985), 2:3ff.